AIKIDO

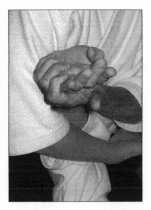

D0770165

AIKIDO

The Peaceful Martial Art

STEFAN STENUDD

BookSurge

Stefan Stenudd is a 6 dan Aikikai Swedish aikido instructor, member of the Swedish Aikikai Grading Committee, the Swedish Budo Federation Board, and the International Aikido Federation Directing Committee. He is also an author, artist, and historian of ideas. He has published a number of books in Sweden, both fiction and non-fiction. Among the latter is an interpretation of the Chinese classic *Tao Te Ching*, and of the Japanese samurai classic *Go Rin no Sho* by Miyamoto Musashi. His novels explore existential subjects from stoneage drama to science fiction, but lately stay more and more focused on the present. He has also written some plays for the stage and the screen. In the history of ideas he studies the thought patterns of creation myths, as well as Aristotle's *Poetics*. He has his own extensive website, which contains a lot of aikido material, among other things:
www.stenudd.com

Also by Stefan Stenudd:
Aikibatto: Sword Exercises for Aikido Students, 2007.
Cosmos of the Ancients: The Greek Philosophers on Myth and Cosmology, 2007.
All's End, 2007.
Murder, 2006.

Cover: *Sankyo*, an aikido pinning technique. Photo by Stefan Stenudd. Design by Stefan Stenudd and Jonas Dahlqvist.

This book was originally published in Sweden, 1992, with the title *Aikido – den fredliga kampkonsten*. This revised edition is written in English by the author.

Aikido: The Peaceful Martial Art
Copyright © Stefan Stenudd, 2008
Book design by the author.
All rights reserved.
ISBN: 978-1-4196-5879-2
Library of Congress Control Number: 2006911077
Publisher: BookSurge Publishing
North Charleston, South Carolina
www.booksurge.com
1-866-308-6235

For additional copies:
www.amazon.com

The secret of aikido is to harmonize ourselves with the movement of the universe and bring ourselves into accord with the universe itself. He who has gained the secret of aikido has the universe in himself and can say: "I am the universe."

Morihei Ueshiba (1883-1969), founder of aikido.

PHONE: TOKYO (03)3203—9236
FAX: TOKYO (03)3204—8145

AIKIKAI
AIKIDO WORLD HEADQUARTERS
17-18 WAKAMATSU-CHO, SHINJUKU-KU
TOKYO 162, JAPAN

November 18, 1992

Dear Sir,

Thank you very much for your new book.

Although I am unable to read the language itself, I find the book to be a magnificent literary work.

I pay my respects to your sincere attitude toward pursuing the truth of Aikido and hope your career as a writer will be more successful in the future.

Doshu sends his kind regards.

Yours truly,

Moriteru Ueshiba
Executive Director
Aikido Hombu Dojo

Greeting from Moriteru Ueshiba, present doshu of aikido, at the publication of the first Swedish edition of this book in 1992.

Contents

The author (to the left) doing some kind of kokyunage in Järfälla, Sweden, 1975. This was where he started with aikido in 1972, at age 18.

Aikido is true

I was seventeen when I first heard about the remarkable Japanese martial art aikido. It was Krister, a friend some years my senior, who told me that he had practiced it.

Just how seriously he regarded aikido, I understood partly from how long he had taken to reveal his knowledge of it – although he must be convinced that it would impress a teenage boy – and partly from his elaborate and solemn way of talking about it. What Krister described was something completely different from a series of tricks to defeat an opponent of twice one's own size, also something different from the concept of athletics for a sound mind in a sound body. What Krister described was a way of living – an art, a philosophy, and yes, kind of a religion.

After listening with widening eyes to Krister's equally fascinating and incomprehensible elaboration on the subject,

The author in 1981, showing the technique yonkyo at the dojo in Brandbergen, Sweden, which he started the same year.

I had to make him show me just how it worked. Also with this he was remarkably reluctant. When I had repeated my wish over and over, he accepted and showed me one of the simpler techniques, *nikyo*, wherein my wrist was turned in such a way that I fell to the floor in sudden pain.

My wrist hurt as if broken, although it was unharmed, and surely my knees had been bruised from the sudden fall to the floor, but I was overcome by one thing only: the beauty of the technique. Krister had only turned his hand around mine, as simply as a butterfly sitting on a straw of grass gently flaps its wings. That was all. And I fell to the floor as abruptly as if I had been hit with a blacksmith's hammer.

It was delightful, in the midst of the pain. It was magical, and incomprehensible although it looked so simple. This I wanted to learn. When the beginners course started in the fall, I showed up in my blue gym suit, anxious and excited.

Like a darkening sky, where one star after the other becomes visible to the eye, aikido has through the years revealed increasing riches to me. Yet I think that the teenage boy, who fell suddenly to the floor by Krister's nikyo, really

The author in 1994, doing taninzugake, several attackers, at his present dojo in Malmö, Sweden. Photo by Ulf Lundquist.

saw absolutely everything that the years of training have since made me acquainted to. Everything was present in that first, painful encounter. What followed was neither more nor less than confirmation – delightful confirmation.

However exotic some of the aikido movements may be, they are permeated by a sense of recognition. When you pull it off all right, and the technique works somewhat, it is not at all like a foreign term you have finally learned by heart, after hours of repetition. No, it's an old friend making his entrance, or a small muscle that has rested for a long time but is once again put to work. All the secrets of aikido are *dèja vu* – they are recognizable from within.

How can this be? Maybe we must say like Plato that man cannot learn anything he did not essentially know from the beginning. All wisdom is contained in our heads from the very moment of birth. We only have to be reminded of it. That is not a bit more odd than the thesis that something must come out of something, never out of nothing.

Such a conception of reality is not strange to me, but more precisely I do, from within, perceive it so that the recognition springs from one firm condition: What I can initi-

The author at a seminar in Stockholm, Sweden, in 2007. Uke, on the right, is Mathias Hultman, 3 dan Aikikai. Photo by Magnus Burman.

ally recognize and see clearly, no matter how little I have practiced it, is true.

What is true, completely true, is immediately recognized by every human being – if he or she just wants to. So, if my senses were at all to be trusted, I knew from the first moment: aikido is true.

Stefan Stenudd

Morihei Ueshiba (1883-1969), founder of aikido, makes a throw without body contact. Among aikidoists, he is usually called kaiso, founder, or Osensei, great teacher. Photo courtesy of Yasuo Kobayashi.

Aikido principles

The impossible martial art

Budo is the collective name for all the Japanese martial arts, such as *judo* (wrestling), *karatedo* (punches and kicks), *kendo* (fencing), *iaido* (solo sword exercises), *kyudo* (archery), *jodo* (staff), and many more. Aikido also has its origin in Japan, and shares a number of traits with other types of budo.

Certainly, each of the Japanese martial arts has its own technical and theoretical characteristics, but also with this in mind aikido has got a place all its own. Most of the aikido characteristics happen to be negations: In aikido there is no competition, no attack techniques, no opponent, no force needed, no shortcut possible. It is difficult to learn, also in its most basic movements, and few are those who have learned to master aikido or parts thereof – even after having studied it for decades.

So, it makes sense to regard aikido as close to impossible. The way is long between the short moments when one's movements don't feel clumsy, and even longer until there are moments where one also feels in harmony with the movements of one's training partner. Therefore it is of some surprise that there are at all people who try it.

Well, those who stick to aikido – and they are not overwhelmingly many – seem to be attracted to the difficulties and all the negations mentioned above. Our modern world offers all too many trophies that are easily caught, with glimmering surfaces but grayish content. You soon learn to set your hope to those surfaces that do not glimmer, even to the point of almost being repulsive. Perhaps they have a very different content.

Although aikido has a number of techniques and forms of training, these visible things are just the tip of the iceberg.

It is the content that is really vast, and makes the training increasingly difficult, the more one progresses. The beginner might sense it, but has no chance of realizing the complexity of aikido. It shows itself gradually, like a landscape opens and widens, the higher the altitude is from which it is observed.

Aikido people
Of those who try one aikido class, a minority returns for a second class, and only a few continue after one semester. On the other hand, those few tend to keep aikido for the rest of their lives – without ever feeling that they master the art, without ever getting fed up with its content. This group is one of its very own kind.

Probably, any hobby or sport tends to gather people who are of similar character. That might even be one of the most important functions of a collective pastime, no matter what its nature is. Nonetheless, aikido attracts its own kind of people. If this were not the case, aikido would soon lose its nature.

We live in a world where we are crowded with much more people than we are able or willing to get to know. In anthropology, man is seen as a flock animal. During most of our history, we have lived in small societies with about eighty individuals or less. That's what we are configured for. The modern world forces us instead to live in great herds, as if we were sheep.

Many of the emotional disturbances in the psyche of modern man stem from this situation. Unconsciously, we strive to surround ourselves with a group of people that is similar to the little flock, and we try to ward off the rest of the world and its population.

Therefore, we need methods to find those smaller groups, preferably those that contain people we can relate to, people who are similar to us – maybe even sibling souls, if that is possible. The more odd a pastime is, the more homogenous a group will gather in it. The exact nature of that homogeneity can be hard to perceive, but it is there.

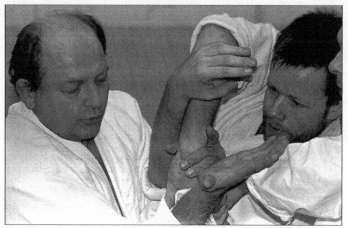

Jan Hermansson, 7 dan Aikikai shihan, shows sankyo on two attackers. He went to Japan already in 1965 to practice aikido. Photo by Ulf Lundquist.

People who practice aikido usually describe themselves as dreamers, and contemplative minds. They never choose words as athlete or fighter. Although they train a martial art, they usually regard themselves as pacifists, and violence has no place in their hearts. Accordingly, the ideal in aikido is not to win in battle, but to prevent it from at all commencing – yes, to do away with violence itself.

Aikido is definitely much more than a sport, and as a martial art it is more about peace than about war. Its practitioners, although far from perfect, are proof of this.

Three years on a stone

In Japan it is a well-known fact that at the outset the student has no way of knowing what the teacher can give, nor if the teacher's methods are the most suitable. It takes three years, they say, for the student to learn enough to decide if the teacher suits him or her. Only at that point, the student is mature enough to choose whether to stay with that teacher, or leave to find another.

The one who makes that decision before three years have passed is bound to get lost. If you hurry on from teacher to teacher, from one art to the other, you will never learn anything more than what you knew to begin with. You cannot see more. For such a student, the most impressive teacher is the one whose ability is the closest to that of the student, and the finest art is the one showing no more than the student is already familiar with.

At first, we can only have an inkling of higher qualities, and it is precisely this vague sense that is the only trustworthy guide for the beginner. We go where we are tempted by our vague sense, our intuition, and we remain there until we fully understand what compelled us to go there. Then we can move on, if we like.

That should take something like three years.

An old Japanese proverb says: "Even on a stone – three years." It means that even something as seemingly simple as sitting down on a stone takes three years to learn. If you can concentrate on each task in life with this insight, with this willingness to study diligently – then you are sure to gain impressive abilities.

The proverb actually admits that after those three years, you really can sit on a stone. Many teachers, who want to bind their students with lifetime contracts, are reluctant to reveal this consequence of the proverb. Keeping the students in a state of confusion might benefit the teacher who has no higher thoughts about his or her own abilities. Students caught in this type of web don't learn much even in thirty years.

It would be going too far to say that anything could be learned in three years. Certainly not aikido. But when that period is completed, one should be able to ascertain how much is to be found in that which has been studied. You have neither become an equal to your teacher, nor a master of your art, but you can envision how far your teacher and your art can take you on the path of life.

Jan Nevelius, 6 dan Aikikai, showing futaridori kokyuho, a breath throw on two attackers, at a demonstration in Stockholm. Photo by Magnus Hartman.

Mouliko Halén, 6 dan Aikikai, showing kokyunage, also a breath throw, at the same demonstration in Stockholm. Photo by Magnus Hartman.

No opponent, no battle

The aikido training itself is quite clear in form. One trainee is the attacker, and one the defender. The former uses grips, strikes, or any of the many weapons in the martial arts. The latter applies the evasive movements of aikido.

The attack techniques are not aikido. They may be borrowed from other martial arts, or simply grips and strikes that need not to have been cultivated into an art. Only the defense is aikido. This defense is not to be done with any aggression, or with the intent of forcing an opponent to submit. It is not done to gain victory. Aikido states that if there is a winner, there are actually two losers.

The aikido techniques should have the trait of endless pliancy, mildly leading the attacking force past its target to a gentle end, where nobody has been harmed. They should be done in a peaceful spirit, as if a battle never occurred, protecting both the attacker and the defender from harm.

Ideally, a bystander is convinced that the whole thing is prearranged between the attacker and the defender, that it is all make-believe. The attacker should all through the technique feel that what happens is exactly what was the initial intent of the attack.

Completion
A good way of describing aikido is that it does not redirect an attack, but helps it to completion. The person who trains aikido not to control his or her own movements, but to perfect those of the attacker, has a far advanced grace in his or her movements. Therefore it makes sense in aikido not to talk about opponent, but partner. Aikido should be equally rewarding to both participants.

Such an ideal leaves no room for competition. The premise of competition is that the advantage of one is the disadvantage of another. Two persons cannot profit equally, or reach the same goal. Actually, in competition the two participants strive to make their opponent as weak and clumsy as possible. That attitude increases a conflict instead of solving it, and hardens the technique instead of softening it. One person's progress is limited by the ability of the opponent. For aikido, this limit is far too narrow. If both participants cooperate instead, they can help each other to advance far beyond the sum of their capacities.

You take turns. First, one is the attacker, and then the other. A correct attack demands intense energy and force, but the defense should be done in a relaxed and yielding manner. The indomitable attack meets a submissive defense. The straight line of the attack is led into a curve, which ends right where the attack commenced. The force returns to its origin, and nothing at all has happened. The movement is not at all a battle, but a dance – a smooth waltz without collision, without any trial of strength.

Natural movement
It is also important not to regard the techniques as counter moves, defensive reactions to sudden charges. The aikido techniques are curves and spirals that constantly move within the trainee – and in the space around him or her.

It is similar to how the dance is hidden within the melody and rhythm of the music. What the attacker is doing is simply inviting to the dance. The movements appear naturally from the music constantly being there, and from the initial step of the partner.

The music of aikido is the flow of energy, an ever-present movement in our living cosmos. If there were no movement, there would be no life. Life is movement. Existence is movement. Aikido opens up to this constant movement, and joins with it. The techniques should be as natural as the fundamental movement of nature.

This movement is harmonious. Huge celestial bodies spin around each other in ellipses. Atoms vibrate in the incomprehensible void. Hundreds of animal species inhabit one little grove. Of course it happens that they collide, with our without intention, but each sector of nature is mostly signified by balance, a friction-free order between all things.

The seemingly random pattern of all these small movements continuously strives for peace and calm, no matter how crowded a space is.

Everything moves, always. There is no one who starts it, nor anyone who finishes it. The whirls of movement are never interrupted. They flow everywhere and always. The only thing that happens in aikido training is that two persons occasionally manifest these whirls. Of course there can be no winner or loser, nor any initiator, in this continuum.

The attacker tries to violate or interrupt the natural, harmonious movement, and needs to be gently returned to it. To seek conflict is to get lost in the movement of nature – and that is only possible when one has lost the connection with one's own natural movement. The aikido techniques have no other purpose than to lead the one astray back to the track of his or her own movement.

The right way of doing an aikido technique is in a spirit of it already having been done. Since it is nothing else than to return the partner to the natural state, there are just two moments: before, when everything was as it should be, and afterward, when everything is again as it should. It is just like supporting one who stumbles, or waking up one who has dozed off. Each time the movement commences, it has already been completed. So there is no way of interrupting it.

The natural movement is ever-present and omnipotent. Therefore, to resist it, like in an attack, is immensely demanding. But to guide the attack back to harmony is just restful. The one who attacks a harmonious person tries to disrupt the natural order, and cannot succeed. The one who avoids the attack and returns the attacker to balance is not doing anything else than following the natural laws, and cannot fail. One only has to realize that – and to live it.

Morihei Ueshiba's path

Everything that moves changes – also aikido. It is visible on anyone who has started to learn it. Although it must be one and the same ideal that attracts the beginners to the training, they are soon caught up in initial limitations of their bodies and minds, and are for a time stuck with an aikido that is but a fraction of what it can become.

They are not alone in this. Each one – also the founder of aikido – has gone through the same. The development is bound to follow the evolving tempers of age and maturity. Morihei Ueshiba, who developed aikido from several traditional martial arts during the first half of the 20th century, showed in his own progress what everyone who trains aikido must go through.

He started as a weak boy of 14 years, frustrated by seeing his father being harassed by bigger and stronger men. Young Morihei was both shorter and more fragile than most. Through diligent martial arts training, he wanted to become strong enough to strike back. He got that strong, and then some. The intense and dedicated training eventually made him so superior that he found no satisfaction in defeating past antagonists. He gained rarely equaled power, and had a hard time finding his superior, so how could he justify assaulting those who were helpless against him?

Furthermore, the martial arts had revealed quite different essences than those of sweet revenge and victory. Within the thousand years old traditions of the martial arts were seeds to very different values. They captured his interest. Morihei Ueshiba discovered this with great surprise when one day in 1925 he was challenged by an officer who wanted to test his ability. Instead of meeting the officer's charges with even more aggression and force, he evaded the attacks again and again. Finally, the officer had spent all his energy on forceful attacks that never hit their target. He had to sink to the ground and give it up.

At that moment, aikido was born to Morihei Ueshiba,

Osensei Morihei Ueshiba in his late years. Photo courtesy of Yasuo Kobayashi.

Aikido 23

who was 41 years of age. Still, the martial art he started to teach was not completely in line with that discovery. Certainly, it started with the evasive movement, but only to follow up with violently felling the opponent to the ground. Ueshiba had great power, so any attacker was thrown far. There was a softness that other martial arts were lacking, which led again and again to young fighters doubting and then challenging him, but they all met a more sudden end to their attempts than the officer had done.

In the 1930's, when Morihei Ueshiba was in his fifties, his physical power was at its zenith. Nobody could stop him or beat him. He was like an Olympic athlete. But time passed for him as for them – although slower. In the 1950's, when he had passed 70 years of age, another kind of aikido emerged. He was still quite invincible, but more so in the way he had dealt with the angry officer thirty years ago. Physical power and resistance were substituted by something similar to the soft force of the wind. His techniques became vague, showing no other force than that of the attacker. Ueshiba's aikido gave the impression of the ageing man, but had the interior of the lively child. Because he was never in the way, he was impossible to fell.

In the 1960's, when his life approached the end, his movements became even subtler. Primarily, his timing changed. His aikido became syncopated, like in music. It started so early that it often seemed to precede the attack completely. If aikido is a way of leading the attacker back to natural harmony and peace, Ueshiba did so at the very moment the attack became an idea in the partner's head. He did not make his techniques on the partner's body, but with his or her intention. The techniques became like abstractions. A sweeping movement with his hand at the very moment when the partner felt the impulse to attack, and the partner would fall. Often they did not even touch. Ueshiba became a mirror, reflecting the partner's attack as quickly as it emerged. Speed was not a problem, since in a mirror it is that of light itself.

One could say that Ueshiba's aikido became guiding

gestures, so that the partner immediately made the technique on himself. Ueshiba must have felt himself one with the harmonious movement of nature. Just showing this wholeheartedly to the partner was enough to halt the attack, and swiftly return the partner to the natural calm. That is one way of describing it – but to do it is quite another matter.

Water, air, and vacuum

Although few of us can claim to progress as spectacularly as Morihei Ueshiba did, I get the impression that every aikido student tends to head toward the same refinement. We go through stages in our aikido, surely with differing speed and amplitude – but without skipping any of those stages. Even mild mannered beginners want to show power and capability through the aikido techniques. They want to throw swiftly and far, fell the biggest opponent, and overwhelm the force of the attack with their own. That is not aikido, but I doubt that anyone can find a shortcut past this phase.

The power that the beginner cannot resist showing off, is the same as that of the attacker. At this level, the aikido techniques are tricks by which the power of the defender surpasses that of the attacker. Here, aikido is like a weapon, a technical advantage. The defender utilizes it with a similar rebellion against the order of nature – vaguely camouflaged by the ethics of self-defense – as that of the attacker. By necessity, it is on this level that every competition sport must stagnate. The attacker and the defender are essentially doing the same thing.

At the next level, they slide apart. This commences when the aikido student has reveled so much in his capacity that he no longer feels proud of it.

The time this takes to reach differs considerably between people, and has nothing to do with what they claim verbally. Oddly, it is my experience that those who speak the most words about softness and pliability take the longest to express this ideal in their movements. Instead, they see their words as an alibi, or as cosmetics on how they actually do their aikido, as if words ruled reality to the extent that they could change it.

What George Orwell called "newspeak" in his novel 1984, is familiar to many a tongue. If we repeatedly call freedom unfree, we might stop longing for it. If the hard is called soft, and the aggressive is called peaceful – then it may become true.

No. The only minds that might be fooled are those whose mouths indulge in newspeak. Probably not even they. Real softness and pliability are evident to every eye, and even more obvious to the attacker. The one who still clings to showing his strength can have movements that are as rounded and evasive as those that are truly soft, but they are harder on the partner, who will feel defied and subdued. Really pliable aikido is not a centrifuge that the attacker is forced into, but a fresh wind that surrounds him, and discretely leads his movements to a harmless ending. At such an ending, no one has been subdued or rebuked.

Water

It can be compared to the elements of nature. The beginner is at first like stone – immovable, tense, with sharp edges. Next comes wood – supple, softening, though still almost immovable. When the beginner finally loosens the feet's panicky contact to the floor, and moves about freely, able to do the techniques with the momentum given by this free movement – then he or she has become like water.

There is great satisfaction at this stage, as well as an impressive ability. The techniques flow. Attackers fall like bowling pins, whether they come one after the other or several at once. You can do your aikido for a long time, without losing control or energy. Therefore it is tempting to remain at this stage, and to convince yourself that the goal is reached. If so, you no longer train to throw away the imperfect and renew your aikido from the ground, but only to polish the abilities you have acquired.

But water is not the softest, not the most yielding. A tiny creek drills through a mountain. Ocean waves throw around ships of any size. Even the rain can strike so hard that people need to escape it. The power of water is great, but its pliability is moderate. That is not enough in aikido.

Air

The most humble of elements is air, which gives room for all the others. Air embraces without pushing, and adapts without resisting. Where water immediately shows its reluctance, the power of air is such that it increases only according to our own speed. Not until we defy it does its capacity become clear to us, and only to the extent we choose to challenge it. Certainly the wind can grab us, sometimes even our houses. But it does not pursue. It passes, and spares that which yields. Water is not as merciful when it flows over us. If we were fish, things would be different, but since that is not our nature, we do wisely to behave more like air.

In aikido this means softness without an underlying threat or spite. We should be adaptive to the terms of the attacker, according to the attack, so that the partner is made aware of no other force behind the movement than his or her own. The one attacked is not in the way, and does not take over the command. The attacker is not subdued. Instead, the attack is helped along the way, to the extent that it merrily rushes ahead and lands somewhere else than initially intended.

When aikido becomes like air, the only obvious force is that of the attacker. The techniques can sweep away so that they stretch over the whole *dojo*, training hall, and be so overwhelmingly grand that walls bulge. But no one is subdued. The partner's force is released instead of smothered.

The joyous dance that follows would no doubt do as an honorable goal for aikido. The aikidoist who has reached this far is fascinating. Also, we have by now gone through

Two Swedish aikido seniors, Lennart Larsson and Lennart Inedahl, practice ikkyo. Photo by Magnus Hartman.

the basic three states of matter: from solid, to liquid, to gas. There is a fourth state of matter, plasma, and there is also another state to be reached in aikido.

Vacuum
Even air makes a certain resistance, although ever so vaguely. It also forces, it also has a kind of surface, and it has its terms that it is reluctant to give up. In air, too, it is possible to feel and recognize an enemy, a target for aggression. True, one cannot really win over air, neither beat nor constrain it, but one can become aware of its identity, and thereby challenge it. If aikido is to make battle impossible, and do away with aggression itself, then air is not the answer. What is next?

Vacuum. Empty space has no body, no substance whatsoever. Still, there is no force great enough to conquer it, no fire to burn it, no power to threaten it, and no room too big to be filled by it, or too small to fit it. Emptiness is the only thing invulnerable, and it is everywhere – between the heavenly bodies in the macrocosm, and between the atoms in the microcosm.

Although it does not act out any will at all, it immediately destroys what challenges it. If the astronauts were not encapsulated in their spaceships and spacesuits, it would instantly rip their lives out of them. Empty space is so completely open, so limitlessly compliant, that every living thing succumbs to it. An attack is totally futile, even lacking a target. There is no substance that makes it possible to persist against such a foe.

Just thinking about attacking is difficult. The only thing needed for such a thought to disappear is to be reminded of the emptiness of space. That drains every fighter of his strength, and cools any anger in an instant.

When aikido becomes like empty space, the attacker will immediately lose all his power, as clearly and suddenly as if his legs were swept away. An attack must have a target to aim at. Emptiness can be no target. Therefore the attacker loses his power at the exact moment when he tries to direct it toward this nothingness. The one who is connected to his or her emptiness only needs to show that vacuum, and the attacker will fall down, drained of energy. The evasive techniques are gone. A never-ending nothingness replaces them. The attack dies at the moment it is initiated.

If you show your vacuum at the moment the attacker takes aim at you, he will lose his stability, and stumble helplessly around. If you are constantly open, showing your vacuum, it becomes impossible for others to even consider attacking you.

Emptiness is not a trick. Someone who just wants the optimal self-defense technique cannot utilize it. Nobody can resist emptiness, including the one who expresses it. It has to be done wholeheartedly, so that you give yourself over to it completely. Therefore, not even at the core of your being do you feel something of substance, worth defending. Emptiness is to deplete oneself, to give up oneself, like afore death. Only if you feel bodiless, without any substance that can be affected by other powers, the attacker will feel the same. The one who gives in to emptiness and becomes vacuum no longer perceives what in him or her can be the target of an attack. Therefore, nobody else can perceive it.

Of course, the aikido of emptiness has nothing to do with techniques and patterns of movement. Anyone watching is unable to see what is going on. The attacker can experience it – but only as something that happens exclusively within him. He loses control, like somebody passing out, and loses power, like after hard work on an empty stomach. He forgets his intention, like snapping out of a daydream.

If the attacker becomes aware that it is the person in front of him creating this, then it is not total emptiness. The attacker should not perceive any other will than his own, and no other explanation to his failure than his own insufficiency.

Spectators can believe nothing else than that such aikido is prearranged. In their minds, the attacker must only be pretending to charge, and then throwing himself. The attacker, too, is unable to explain it in any other way.

In the aikido of emptiness, the aikidoist has become invisible, like nonexistent. Everything moves within and around the partner. Self-defense has ceased to be an ingredient. Threat and violence fade away. Only at this stage, a serenity that reaches beyond one's own mind can be achieved. The surroundings are seduced by it, like delight is awakened at the scent of a precious flower.

Maybe some other kind of aikido comes after that – who knows? Although that is hard to imagine, you should not take it as an argument for interrupting your quest, and settling down. At the moment when you believe yourself to have reached the goal, you are doomed to start closing your gates, to stiffen, and begin to wither. Also emptiness, you have to try to throw away and desert. Otherwise it is impossible to discover if anything else lies beyond it.

Bewildered and amazed. Children's class in Brandbergen, Sweden. Photo by Gunilla Welin.

Sooner like the youth

It is a common view among aikido instructors that the eso-teric forms of aikido are best suited for older practitioners. They think that young aikidoists do better to show off their energy and speed, since that is what suits their age. Not until the years have made the joints stiffen and the movements shrink, should one turn toward an aikido soft as air, and only when the grave is around the corner should one pass over to the aikido that shows emptiness – if one is able to.

Certainly, youthful vigor makes it difficult to turn away from what seems powerful, to be mild as the wind. The young prefer to test their limbs with such force that they almost crack, and to throw their partners to the mat so hard that it whips up clouds of dust. I don't think that there is a teacher born who can make youngsters abandon such games. But we lie about aikido if we say that they should remain in this state until they have lost the power to pull it off. If that is true, then the aikido of air is weaker than that of water, and the aikido of emptiness is the weakest of them all. That is not true.

Also those who start with aikido in early childhood are able to sense another force than that of muscles, and they desire it. This is particularly true about the youngest ones, who don't let curiosity be overpowered by pride. Telling them to wait and remain in a more primitive form of aikido just because they have not reached a senior age, is nothing but a sin. When people want to pass from a lower to a higher state, we should not try to stop them – but cheer them on.

Sin in training

Behind the term in the Bible translated as 'sin', are three Hebrew concepts. They all have to do with traveling toward a goal, like the arrow heading for the target. One such sin is slowing down on the way to the target, another to take unnecessary roundabouts, and a third to steer away from it. So, what the Old Testament regards as sin is not to hurry as swiftly and straight for the goal as one is able.

Applied to aikido, this means that the beginner of whatever age should be allowed to explore every stage he or she reaches, and to delight in it. It also means that the beginner should be encouraged to move on upward, to the next height, and then the next. Just as it is possible for the teacher to pull the student through the stages in a higher tempo than the student would manage on his own, it is inappropriate for the teacher to have any opinion about what that speed should be. You can only wish it to be high, and that along the way the student will not pause more than needed to gain energy for the next challenge.

The opinion that there is a proper time for everything, is mostly supported by those who wish to remain in a stage they should be mature enough to leave behind. Just as each age in human life has its costs as well as rewards, at every phase of one's development one must desert something in order to achieve something else. Sometimes, it hurts to give this something up. You might hesitate for the very simple reason that you know what you have, but not what you can get. Unfortunately, he who gets stuck in such a sin prefers to pull others to him, instead of allowing them to pass.

Osensei on film

Morihei Ueshiba, the founder of aikido, is an excellent model to follow, but he is used and interpreted in many different ways. Many want to make him an unreachable ideal, a saint on top of a high pedestal. In their eyes it is almost rebellious trying to learn an equally advanced aikido as that of the founder.

I am not at all sure that he regarded himself as that elevated. If he did, why would he at all have cared to teach his art? Morihei Ueshiba pushed his students along. He was full of explanations and instructions, though they were not always understandable to his students. If we regard him as a discoverer and a breaker of new ground in the martial arts, then the only thing that makes sense is not to halt after his demise, but endeavor to continue where he left off. We should hurry all we can toward the aikido that Ueshiba was able at the time of his death, and move on from there.

I think it is possible. At least I know that it is impossible if we do not try.

Morihei Ueshiba was filmed now and then, through the years. On these films, the development of his aikido is as clear as day. In the earliest known filming of his aikido, from 1935, his strength is considerable, and his techniques are at least as sudden and rough as the attacks. No matter how many opponents throw themselves at him, they are thrown back with even more force. But in the last films, recorded in the 1960's, he does little more than walk around making gentle gestures with his hands, sort of waving at his attackers. This alone makes them fall – at the moment they get ready to charge.

There are many aikidoists who hold the 1935 film as their favorite. There, anybody can see what a mighty fighter Ueshiba was. They tend to shun the last films, which give them feelings of confusion and doubt. What he shows there can't be possible, can it? Isn't it just an old man, surrounded by obliging assistants? So, his aikido became such that even aikidoists started to think that all was prearranged.

In my eyes, those last films are by far the most fascinating and appealing. They show an art that could be explanatory, maybe even give meaning to life. So why not hurry there, as quickly as we can?

The spirits of ages
It is indeed possible to compare the stages of aikido with the ages of man, but we should not demand of people to follow these intervals slavishly, like prison terms. People are so different and unpredictable that we can expect some children to show the form of emptiness, and some aged people to stick to the aikido of rocks. In that way, advanced aikido and people are the same: They don't fit into one single mold, but are unforeseeable by nature. Actually, I would say that in his last days, the age group Ueshiba looked like the most was that of the youth. Not physically, certainly, but in spirit.

One can glimpse, like a contour, how the spirit of each age group is.

Children are by nature open-minded, swallowing the claims of their teachers without even tasting them first. They don't spare themselves the least when they try the path of aikido.

For the adults, it's not that simple. They have prestige and preconceptions, which they cherish firmly. They are reserved when listening to a teacher, wary of being lured into other thoughts than they had to begin with, and reluctant to discover things, the values of which they cannot at first calculate. Often they are so cornered by their self-esteem that they are unable to learn anything at all. What they manage at the most is by practice to reach some or other skill. They are pleased with this, as if they already knew all about what life could give.

It can take well into their old age before they open up, and if so, with a feeling very close to that of youth.

No doubt, youngsters are often mesmerized by the sim-

Instructor in a jam. Children's class in Brandbergen, Sweden. Photo by Gunilla Welin.

pler aspects of aikido, and can gorge on pure bodily achievements such as strength, stamina, and tempo. But only their bodies focus on that. Their spirits are usually completely different. Youthful minds have an unlimited thirst for life, and they are obsessed by what is probably the most important human trait: curiosity.

Fascination

A child quickly loses interest, and lets the mind fly around like a snow fling in the wind, but a youth can spend all the time and energy on one and the same thing, as long as his or her fascination is aroused. Adults start by asking how they can get out of things, or how they can keep their daily order undisturbed, whereas youths plunge into unknown deep waters without a single sting of apprehension.

Fascination is probably the answer. Youths allow themselves to be fascinated – by charismatic idols, by the biological mechanisms of reproduction, or by a peaceful Japanese martial art.

Fascination is their battery, and the playground slide they throw themselves into. That is an excellent attitude for making grand discoveries in aikido. Instead of trying to halt the youth who rushes forward, adults would do better to join – or to step out of the way. Only those who allow themselves to be amazed by aikido can ever reach an aikido that is amazing.

Female advantage

In this book, when grammar has forced me to specify gender, I have either used both 'he' and 'she', or just 'he' for the sake of simplicity. In no way does it mean that men are more suited for aikido. Not at all. Aikido makes no difference between the sexes.

Already in the early 20th century, Morihei Ueshiba had several female students, who trained with the men on equal terms, and reached just as impressive skills. That is still the case. Men and women train together without any complications, and they develop their skills according to personal conditions that have nothing to do with gender.

Yet, if we must generalize, with some hesitation it can be said that one sex has a slight advantage over the other: the women. This depends on the nature of aikido. Boys and men have a habit of flexing their muscles, and leap into battle with stubborn pride and a hunger for victory. This is far from the ideal of aikido. Women tend to prefer a gentle approach, the softer way, yielding instead of confronting, and following rather than leading. That's a superior basis for advanced aikido.

So, although more men than women train aikido, this female advantage is frequently visible on the aikido mat. Women rarely have the same need for self-confirmation that many men are victims of, so they have a shortcut to an aikido filled with tenderness, generosity, and benevolence. That's a splendid advantage.

Tantodori, knife defense, at Iyasaka dojo, Stockholm. Åsa Scherrer, 4 dan Aikikai, practicing with Urban Aldenklint, 6 dan. Photo by Magnus Hartman.

Unfortunately, the same characteristics often make women less willing than men to stand in front of the group and teach. Also, women rarely hurry to try for the next grade. Whereas men are quick – sometimes too quick – to see their own abilities, many women tend to look more at their own shortcomings. For aikido to develop in equality, women need to be confident about their abilities, and men need to actively encourage the women to move boldly ahead.

For the sake of balance and harmony, it is important to be keenly aware of the female qualities – both around and within oneself, no matter what one's gender is.

The latter is particularly important to men doing aikido. When they talk with harsh voices about self-defense practicality and making the technique work against any foe, they express the traditional male role. They need to indulge in the softness of aikido, its yielding and compassionate side, with at least the same enthusiasm. Otherwise they risk making aikido a less peaceful martial art. I have seen symptoms of it in many a dojo.

Another important female advantage is the natural ease by which women find and develop their center, *tanden*. They are not alien to focusing on the abdomen, since that is where they host the very future of mankind. Men tend to work from their shoulders, and often have a very hard time changing to centering their power and techniques in the abdomen.

It is not necessary to speak of different aspects of aikido in terms of gender. Not every man is hard, not every woman soft, and so on. But if we avoid the gender perspective completely, we are probably becoming victims of it.

I would like us to move further. There is a greater percentage of women among beginners, than there are among *yudansha*, those with dan grades. And among *shihan*, the certified teachers with 6 dan or more, I guess the women can still be counted with the fingers of one hand. That is insufficient. We need women to have equal influence in the development of aikido, or there is a great risk that it will not soften but harden.

Maybe there will not be a significant change until we get a female *doshu*, the Aikikai head of aikido. This title is inherited within the Ueshiba family, and I guess that there are about as many girls as boys born within it.

In yo

Another way of looking at it is the old Chinese polarity *yin* and *yang*, in Japanese *in* and *yo*. The former stands for darkness, the earth, and the female, while the latter symbolizes light, heaven, and the male. Originally, the terms refer to the shady and the sunny side – like on a tree, which has one side that the sunshine reaches, and the opposite side not.

In Eastern tradition, the polarity of yin and yang is of fundamental importance. It is used in cosmology, in traditional medicine, and almost every other aspect of life. The ideal is to find balance between the two, as in the classical symbol of yin and yang, the circle divided into two fields, one white and one black – but with a dot of black in the

Yin and yang, the cosmological opposites of Chinese philosophy. Ink by the author.

white, and a similar dot of white in the black. This signifies that nothing is completely yin or completely yang. There is always a mix of the two, though the proportions vary.

Although the Chinese tradition demands balance between the two, it is common to find yang regarded as the superior one. Heaven is seen as the ruler of Earth, light conquers darkness, and so on. There is little in the old Chinese cosmology to support such a preference.

Actually, one of the greatest books of Chinese wisdom, *Tao Te Ching*, expresses quite the opposite: Lao Tzu, its legendary writer, claims yin, the female, to be superior. He praises the low, the yielding, the humble, and other aspects that signify yin, while he warns against many typical yang aspects. He also frequently refers to *Tao*, the first cosmic principle, as the mother.

Aikido is very close to the Taoist ideals. If you are familiar with *Tao Te Ching*, you probably don't need to read any further in this book.

Throw away

Among the tales of old Japan, there is one about the ruler who wanted to master *kyudo*, the art of archery. For that purpose, he sought out the man reputed to be the superior archer in the land. The master was a low-voiced man of modest means. They took a walk on the field behind his simple abode, while the ruler enquired about his skills.

As they walked there peacefully, they heard a passing bird call in the sky above. Immediately, the master had the bow in his hand, and shot an arrow – without even looking in the direction of the bird. It happened as quickly as a thought runs through one's mind. The arrow hit the bird in its chest, and it fell to the ground.

The ruler was aghast. He had never before seen such grace, such swiftness and accuracy, with the bow and arrow.

"You have to be my teacher!" he exclaimed.

But the master shook his head.

"I am a mere beginner at archery. I can't be anybody's teacher."

No matter how the ruler insisted, the master did not change his mind. Instead he said, finally:

"Return in ten years. Maybe by then I will be worthy of teaching you."

The ruler had to settle with this offer, and returned to his castle. But he did not forget the master archer and his splendid display. So, when ten years had passed, the ruler returned to him.

This time too, they took a walk in the field, and the ruler was full of questions about how the master might have increased his skills. Soon, a bird passed above them. The master did not look, but stretched the string of his bow – without an arrow – and released it. The bird twitched, as if hit by an arrow, and fell to the ground.

The ruler had no words for his amazement, but he stated firmly that now, the master had to accept him as a student.

"No, no," the master replied. "I am still a mere beginner."

There was no way of changing his mind. The ruler had to accept another ten years of waiting.

"Maybe by then I will be worthy", the master said.

It so happened that after a few years of unrest, the land got a new ruler, and the old one had to step down from the throne. He escaped alive, but lost all his power and riches. He walked on the streets among his former subjects, and lived in poverty.

One day, as he wandered the streets of the city, he came across a big gathering of people, crowded around an old man, listening in awe to what he had to say. It was the old master of archery. The ruler greeted him with great joy.

"Master," he said humbly, "how far have you reached with your art, after all these years? What wonders can you now accomplish with your bow and arrow?"

The master looked up at him with an expression of confusion, and asked:

"What is a bow, what is an arrow?"

The teacup

In the Japanese martial arts, *budo*, it is well known that you have to throw away your accomplishments, in order to gain new ones. The one who achieves something great and then is unable to let go of it, has no place within himself for additional knowledge.

Achievement easily becomes a prison, where vanity is the attentive guardian. When you have reached a skill worth pride, it is difficult to move on. Ability is a kind of fortune, just as tempting and seductive as gold. If you hold on to every skill, you will soon carry such a heavy load that your legs are unable to take another step.

In Zen, the meditative form of Buddhism, this is compared to having one's teacup filled to the brim. There is no room for another drop of tea in it. He who wants to receive must first empty himself. He who wants to learn must at first forget.

Seishiro Endo, 8 dan Aikiai, teaching at a seminar in Stockholm. He is a prominent teacher at Hombu dojo, Tokyo. Photo by Magnus Hartman.

Usually we assume that if you empty your mind, you never increase your learning. You remain ignorant, even silly. So, most people strive to expand their vessels to contain more. But the vessel has its given volume, and there is a limit to what it can contain. In order to learn something new, you just have to throw away knowledge of old.

Understanding

The fear of emptying one's mind stems from ignorance of the difference between knowledge and understanding. Names of things, measures, and dates, all demand space in our heads to remain there. Also, they demand practice and repetition, not to escape us. But understanding takes no place. What you have once understood cannot escape you, and still takes no space in your head.

Knowledge in itself is something dead. It is when knowledge leads to understanding that it comes to life, and gains meaning. It is also at this moment that knowledge has served its purpose, and might as well wither away – as it is naturally inclined to do. Knowledge wants to fade away. That is why it takes such efforts to keep.

In math, which is a science with all the insights of its high age intact, no problem is regarded as solved until the solution can be proven correct. It is not enough that the student points to a formula in the textbook, and claims that it must be correct to be included. The student has to prove it. Therefore, mathematics is a vital and agile science, although it might be the oldest one. Each new mathematician can trace all its formulas and conclusions all the way back to the logical fundaments of math, which are none other than the logical fundaments of man. Since math can be traced all the way back to its beginning, it can be recreated anytime, by anyone of its practitioners. Then, who is afraid of throwing away knowledge?

Knowledge may be an impressive ingredient in conversation, but it is a burden by nature. As soon as you have reached the goal of your quest, you should throw that burden off. Knowledge is nothing but the fuel that takes us to understanding. When this has been reached, there is no reason to hold on to knowledge.

Simplifications

I was about ten or eleven, when we started to touch on the subject of chemistry in school. We dissolved sugar lumps in cold water, then in hot water, and stuff like that. Our teacher explained the process in the crude way that we were able to grasp. When we reached high school, we got a real chemistry teacher, who immediately declared to us:

"Forget anything they taught you before!"

We had to start over, with the periodic system, atoms, molecules, and so on. There was a whole lot to memorize, until we got to senior high school, where the teacher greeted us with these words:

"Forget everything you learned in junior high!"

So, we had to start all over again. After that, I was not inclined to test chemistry at university level.

On each step of the way we had learned chemistry through simplifications, to have any chance at grasping that complicated science. We needed these simplifications to gradually mature in our understanding of chemistry. Only by this process would we be able to comprehend the intricate theories of chemistry today. It might have been faster to jump directly to the latest discoveries of chemistry at once, if we could only understand them. We could not.

The simplifications worked as steps along the way, but if we had stuck to earlier knowledge, our understanding would not have deepened an inch. We had to throw previous knowledge away. Although it was relevant and sort of correct in its phase, by the next step of the way it was false.

That is how aikido works, as well, though not as evidently. Those who cannot throw away the knowledge of previous phases are trying to build higher understanding on false ground. It does not work.

So, in your learning process, always try to understand, and let knowledge sip away as it naturally tends to do. Why flex one's brain as much as the shoulders in arm wrestling, instead of relaxing and letting knowledge do its task and then be gone? We must trust that our brains have the wisdom to keep the important stuff. We should hold on to the formulas, but throw away the examples.

Unawares
In aikido, the beginner learns to be completely aware of the body, and all the details of the techniques. These are repeated and polished endlessly in practice, and every little flaw is corrected.

In all this labor with the small perspective, the beginner is often unaware of what happens at a larger scale. As he is polishing the basic techniques, his body and mind will naturally and irreversibly absorb the true basis of aikido. Posture, breathing, the flow of energy, and an extended awareness – all this will dawn on him through the practice, unawares, and become natural expressions of his being. This is the essence of aikido. The beginner's movements get a center and a flow, and his mind is opened and cleared while his brain is occupied by all these basic techniques.

Therefore, when your being has become one with the essence of all the techniques, you should throw them away. You can forget them, because now they are inside of you. When you need an aikido technique, you can immediately recreate it.

In the terms of modern natural science, you could say that your aikido has moved from the conscious thought, somewhere in the convolutions of your brain, to the reflexes of the medulla oblongata. Movements no longer demand consciousness, but work on reflex. The relaxed mind acts instantly in the way that fits the situation. You throw away your knowledge and trust that your own being, your body, is prepared to do what is needed, and does it correctly. That is real ability.

This is the aikido path to understanding, and it is the same for any budo. Only the one who dares to forget will learn. The more you dare to leave behind, the more you will find.

To know or to learn

We imagine that the discoveries of the natural sciences are unquestionable truths, and that they progress in a steady march toward greater clarity as to how the world works. That might not be the case. A scientist by the name of Thomas S. Kuhn mapped the development of natural science, and found out that it is not as straight and even as the runway of an airport. Science is developed through sudden revolutions. There is a rather unproductive stagnation between them.

Kuhn talks about *paradigm* and *anomalies*. Each scientific period confesses to a certain paradigm, sort of a basic law for how things studied within that science are supposed to

The author at a Berlin seminar. Photo by Frank Weingärtner.

operate. The paradigm describes what natural laws are to be taken for granted. But reality soon shows deviations from this paradigm. These deviations are called anomalies, and they are phenomena that behave contrary to what they should, according to the accepted natural laws.

When such anomalies pop up, they are not used to question the paradigm. Instead, they are ignored. Scientists hide and deny them in protection of the paradigm, or simply because they are unable to see beyond it. Finally, though, the anomalies are so many and so obvious that they can neither be denied nor hidden. Then a scientific revolution erupts, where the paradigm is thrown in the garbage. A new paradigm is formed, including and explaining the anomalies.

The new order is quickly established, and soon it starts to hide new anomalies that unavoidably appear in time. This periodic process is like building a house, tearing it down, and building a new one on the same lot – again and again. Kuhn found that this seems to happen with surprising regularity. In chemistry, since I mentioned it above, he found that it happens with an interval of about 70 years.

Why this inefficient resistance in the very temples of

Aikido

reason and fact? Why don't the scientists jump at every new anomaly, as soon as it appears? Are they not curious?

The reason is more simple and human than the authorities of science would ever care to admit. They spend a big portion of their lives learning the paradigm, its examples and consequences. They don't want to throw all that away, and start fresh – especially since it gives them no advantage against the young novices who are supposed to be their students. So they hold on hard to their paradigm, and don't care about how far it takes them from reality. They root in the past and try to ban the very future. Since they rule at the universities and the research institutes, they are able to stall the development – but never to avert it completely. Their cardinal error is that they don't want to learn, but to know.

It happens just as easily in aikido.

Positive
Now, aikido around the world is not as homogenous as the natural sciences, and not as controlled. Still, it is quite possible that we might detect paradigms, anomalies, and returning revolutions, also in aikido. Anyway, many practitioners fall into this tempting trap of knowledge.

I believe that those people were stuck in it to begin with. Their teacups were not full at first, but they wanted it done as quickly as possible, and then put a lid on them. They never allow themselves to be surprised, and they are unable to learn anything more than what they could imagine from the beginning. They hurry to pour their knowledge on others, as if by that cementing their paradigm and keeping the anomalies off.

Those who really want to learn behave differently. When something is shown to them, they do not at first compare it to their own insights, in order to dismiss it if there is a mismatch. They try to understand in what way what has been shown can actually be correct. It is a question of being positive contra negative. Afore something strange one should at first ask how it can be – not immediately halt and shout that it is impossible.

Much in aikido can at first seem completely ridiculous – for example moving the whole body away from a strike, instead of just ducking, or relaxing all muscles to get out of a hard grip, instead of forcefully wrenching free. What seems totally wrong in the beginning is indeed wrong at that moment, but by time it becomes more and more correct. You learn.

When you are always prepared to learn, you are open to new solutions, and therefore not afraid of new difficulties. You do not settle with only repeating again and again the techniques you master. Instead you forget them and move on to the things in aikido that you feel the least comfortable with. If a problem appears, if something suddenly does not work, your lust to try and try increases. Then the solution will appear.

Beginners

A clear example of this is when you do aikido techniques on an absolute beginner. The otherwise soft movements tend to become tense, the round forms become jagged, and suddenly there is a technique that just does not work on the beginner, no matter how easily you are able to do it on others. This often depends on the beginner doing the attack incorrectly – for example passively, like someone who does not mean it, or stiffly, like the one who is sure that there is no risk involved.

Still, you should not hasten to blame the complication on the beginner, and settle for the awkward way the technique comes out, or rush on to other techniques in search for one that works. Use the opportunity. Question what happened. Did the beginner really attack incorrectly, and if so, what was his or her mistake? Is it possible to do harmonious aikido on this attack, even though it is faulty, and if so, how? Maybe there was no significant error in the attack, but it revealed a shortcoming of yours.

Aikido is created to work against the best attacks, those most skilled and definite. This still does not mean that aikido is helpless against an inferior attacker. With aikido, you

Seminar in Plzen, Czech Republic. Photo by Antonín Knízek.

should be able to handle also unskilled attacks. Only after having solved this, or found a way to the solution, should you move on to correcting the attack.

Otherwise every aikidoist will soon be as snared by limits and conditions in the martial art, as the fly is in the spider's web. Those who want to know always start by correcting others, but those who want to learn begin by correcting themselves. Only after that do they correct their partner, if the partner wants them to.

The world is full of proverbs telling that the more you know, the less you understand, and the more you learn, the more remains to be learned, and so on. Although nothing is wrong with these expressions, they do so easily become empty words. Of course there are things we actually learn, and many things we do understand. If our minds are in some order, these things will increase by age. Real wisdom would be to trust that one knows what one knows, and therefore always be willing and able to question it.

Human beings have an enormous number of brain cells, and in addition, deep within, a sort of radar that infallibly recognizes truth. There is no danger in wholeheartedly test-

ing things that are strange to you, and opening up to conflicting explanations. Only if you always do so, can you be
sure that your own truths really stand.

Quantity

Those who hold on hard to their knowledge do by time get
bored, finding little to do. Since they refuse novelties and
changes, they must fill their time with other things. To escape the threats to their knowledge in quality, they turn to
quantity. They increase the number of examples of one and
the same paradigm.

In every kind of budo there is *kata*, a series of predeter-
mined movements. Traditionally, kata training is a good
method of exercising the martial arts basics, with a maximum of concentration and care. You train your kata to perfection, and in this constant repetition you find the gate to
another kind of inspiration, another kind of awareness in
your performance.

But kata can certainly become pure formality. There are
really no solid arguments for learning more than one kata,
as long as it is well composed for its purpose. The more kata
you try to memorize and master, the greater the risk is to get
lost in quantity. You find pride in knowing them all, and at
the same time they are so many that there is no time to train
any one of them sufficiently. None of the kata in this heap
can open any gate. They just become a pile of techniques.

Therefore, in every martial art the number of basic techniques is strictly limited – but the number of variations, to
be born naturally in the moment, is immense. When there
are too many basic techniques, the practitioner's attention
will get stuck on the technical level, and his or her budo will
never come to life.

In aikido you move on by concentrating completely on
what you do at the moment, and then throw it away. You
forget it to concentrate completely on the next thing. That is
being in the present. Precisely because you don't collect and
keep things, there is no limit to what you can perceive.

Here and now

In *kyudo*, Japanese archery, the beginner should have only one arrow in the quiver. Otherwise he or she might think of the next arrow, already when aiming with the first one. You have to be completely focused on what you are in the middle of, what you are doing at the moment. If you allow yourself to be distracted by what preceded it or what comes next, you will have a hard time hitting the target.

Of course, this goes for all that you undertake. The one who is in the process of learning something is sure to make several mistakes along the way. If you allow yourself to let this worry you, it will be twice as difficult for you to progress. Bad performance must be forgotten, not to make the one guilty of it discouraged.

Also good performance can be a hindrance, even for the most experienced, in making him or her worry if it can be repeated.

The optimistic beginner tends to hastily shoot the first arrow, convinced that the next one will do better, and the one after that even more so. He will be a brilliant archer – in his imagination. If he wants this to become reality, he needs to empty the quiver and learn to concentrate on one arrow at a time.

This is far from only a pedagogical trick. It is a basic principle in the Far East.

Nakaima
In Shinto, the old Japanese religion, *Nakaima* is sort of the equivalent of the Judeo-Christian Paradise. Nakaima consists of two words. The first means the middle, which refers to right where you are, right here. The other word means now. If you can live completely in the here and now, settle exactly where you are, and not let anything else distract you, then you are surely in some kind of paradise.

In budo, this is practically identical with emptiness, *ku* or *kara*. When you succeed in forgetting the past, the future,

The author at a seminar in Pardubice, Czech Republic. Photo by Leos Matousek.

and every other place where you are not, you become empty. Everything that happens – even that of your doing – is a surprise. Therefore, nothing can get you off-balance, and nothing can forestall your action. You are immediate in everything.

Already done

The samurai in old Japan had a principle, partly derived from Zen, for how to face danger: You need to enter the battle with the attitude of already being dead. Then you cannot lose. The one who holds on hard to life will be paralyzed by his fear of losing it, and thereby be defeated.

If you can tell yourself that all is already over, that you are already dead, then nothing can distract you. You are here and now, completely unconditional. You are empty, and therefore impossible to predict, dupe, or catch by surprise.

When you learn to strike with the sword in kendo and iaido, or with your fist in karatedo, the best is to say to yourself: It is already done. Then your body, and your inner being, will choose the best moment for the strike, and you

Aikido

will be just as surprised as your opponent. Such strikes can only be avoided by the same kind of empty mind.

Whatever technique you are about to do, whatever situation you are in – if you can feel that everything has already been done, everything is over, then that can neither be stopped nor altered. Such aikido gives the impression of not at all having been done by the aikidoist, but by something else, something higher. If you dare to trust this higher entity, and turn over your actions to it, then you truly get an aikido that challenges no one, but creates peace. It is one with what is natural.

Again, this is not as easy to do, as it is to describe. But it is worth trying, no matter how long it might take to accomplish.

Considering how long we humans have walked the Earth by now, it must be enough with victories that demand defeats of others, advances that demand decline, and people who live at the expense of others. It is worth a lifetime trying to find a way to interact with other people that harms no one, and does not profit one at the cost of another. If you carry this ideal with you, your aikido will eventually not only look like a dance – it will be dancing. A delighted, lively spin. Playful interaction with whoever approaches you.

A shared journey

In Buddhism, there are two ways to salvation: *Hinayana* and *Mahayana*. They can be translated to 'the smaller vessel' and 'the bigger vessel'. They refer to man's voyage from bewilderment to enlightenment, the great assurance.

Hinayana is to be alone in this vessel. This was most common in ancient India. Many a man, reaching middle age, left his home and family to find the way to a grander truth, the meaning of life – before it was time for life to leave him. To this man, eternity and truth were magnitudes that could only be reached by the individual, by his inner incurable solitude.

Mahayana, on the other hand, was sort of a group effort. Several people, who wanted to find the meaning in all this, gathered in the vessel and began their voyage together. Thereby, they could give each other support and advice along the way. They were certain that such great truths as the ones they searched could only be reached through the joint efforts of several humans. The lonely ones get lost, they claimed, but the group leads its members in the right direction.

Surely, a universal truth is to be found somewhere in between these two standpoints. Still, while voluntary solitude definitely excludes the support and help of others, the joint voyage hardly makes an individual private experience impossible. Therefore, Mahayana really seems to be a combination of the two. But it must be admitted, and history has proven it repeatedly, that a group can get just as hopelessly lost as a lonely traveler. Also, it is sometimes difficult for someone on such a quest to find like-minded people to share the vessel. When it comes to the eternal questions, there are no guarantees.

Mahayana budo

Nonetheless, budo is Mahayana. We travel together. He who thinks that the training partners are just tools borrowed for his own development will not be able to take many steps on the way. We have to help each other wholeheartedly, and learn from each other in a continuous exchange.

In budo, the symbol of the mirror is frequently used. The partner is a mirror of my aikido and my frame of mind. The students are mirrors of their teacher's insight and ability.

Since old times it is said that the master shall be judged by the accomplishments of his or her students. That is how to discover real grandeur, as well as embarrassing shortcomings. In addition, no practitioner is better than he or she succeeds to be with the least capable partner. Harmony,

Warm-up exercise at the author's dojo in Malmö, Sweden. Photo by Anders Heinonen.

elegance, and naturalness, should signify the movements of the aikidoist, whoever is the partner.

The techniques are not at all done in order to gain victory, but as tools to exercise harmony and naturalness – for oneself and for one's partner. Both should feel enriched when the technique is completed. As the training progresses, both should get closer to the truth.

Those who enter a dojo only to work on their own development will have a hard time learning anything at all. Someone with this attitude is just too insensitive to discover his own shortcomings or to sense a better way of doing aikido. Such an aikidoist is standing still, and those who train with him will feel discomfort.

In olden times, this would have been described as the budo of death, not of life. It is sufficient for learning how to injure your partner and win one or other battle, but not for giving the partner life and delight. You become a much too hardened blade, which must one day crack. Those who are unable to let go of the thought of self-defense, of becoming invincible, fall into this trap.

Pass it on

In the spirit of Mahayana lies also the revelation that aikido is not something you can buy or steal. You get it as a gift. Aikido is a gift from its founder, Morihei Ueshiba, from his predecessors and successors, from one's own teacher and all one's training partners. The only way to return the favor is to pass the gift on, whether this is done by being a training partner or a teacher.

There is no room for egoism in this. In training, you have to strive to give your partners all that they need, and as a teacher you have to give your students all that you are able. If you are an aikido student, it should be more important that the partner learns and advances, than that you do. If you are an instructor, the goal should be that the students surpass their teacher. The greatest merit for an aikido teacher is to become a student of his or her students.

Mahayana means that until everybody has reached a certain height, none of them has done so.

That self-defense thing

The East Asian martial arts have an air about them that is not altogether sympathetic, nor something to strive for. I refer to the ingredient of violence, of course.

This thing started already when Oddjob crushed interior decorations with "karate chops" in the Bond movie *Goldfinger*, or maybe as early as with the introduction of jiu-jitsu tricks to the west in the beginning of the 20th century. As always with the unknown, rumors took off about the mysterious techniques by which a small man would be capable to fell a tall one. Ever since the budo arts started to be practiced in the west, temperamental persons who want to learn how to fight have visited them. It is not the ideal interest group.

Taisabaki evasion from multiple attackers with bokken, the wooden sword, at a seminar in Plzen. Photo by Antonín Knízek.

So far, aikido has been pleasantly spared those spectacular rumors, and that type of crowd. When wild-mannered men look at the tranquil and relaxed spirit of aikido training, they lose interest and search for other sports. They often lack the patience to sit through the warm-up of an aikido class, and leave before the actual aikido training commences.

Only by the late 1980's, aikido has entered the world of battle on the silver screen, by Steven Seagal's violent adventure movies. There is reason to be ambiguous about this. Seagal's aikido techniques in the movie versions have little to do with the spirit and ideals of aikido. He would probably be the first to admit that.

Aikidoists in disbelief
Apart from what Seagal's fame has brought, aikido is generally known as a form of gentle gymnastics, rather than as self-defense and martial art. Certainly, this is peaceful for the reputation of aikido, but also misleading. For those who wonder: aikido is highly efficient self-defense. Otherwise its principles would be faulty, its movements misdirected, and the whole training would be massive self-deception.

One of the charming things about aikido is that its practitioners don't trust it much as self-defense. Instead they conclude that it is difficult to learn, and their own ability is inadequate. They can't imagine that they would be able to succeed with any of the aikido techniques, were they to face a real threat. Therefore, those who have actually experienced such situations show genuine surprise when telling how they did an aikido technique, out of reflex, and it actually worked.

Generally speaking, the aikido techniques are easier to do on an ignorant attacker, than on training partners in the dojo. The latter are prepared for what will happen, and have a better chance of resisting, if they choose to.

Budo evolution

Aikido is constructed to neutralize the most skilled attacker, just like the old martial arts out of which it was developed. If these techniques and methods had not worked, they would have been forgotten long ago. Traditional budo has evolved in a similar fashion to that of Darwin's natural selection. Those who practiced insufficient disciplines just did not survive the days when the martial arts were indeed martial.

When westerners are eager to rationalize and improve the old budo arts, they forget this development over time. How can one single human being have a better understanding than that of thousands of people through centuries of practical experiences? That is refinement by countless processes of trial and error. So, of course aikido works.

Yet, aikido does its most good as self-defense in the hidden. Long before the practitioners feel that they have gained any technical skills worth trusting, their balance and stability have increased. So has the speed of their reflexes and reactions. They have also learned to utilize their bodily and mental resources much more efficiently. Such abilities are not easy to observe, but they are quite real and important, nonetheless.

When predator males fight over a female, or over leadership of the flock, they rarely harm each other seriously.

They know their powers, and how to hold them back. Pigeons, on the other hand, lack that control. They might pick each other to death in the most trivial fight, because they do not know their power. Those who practice a martial art usually become peaceful for the simple reason that they respect the power and effects of violence, and want to avoid them. Also rather hot-tempered persons tend to calm down through training, and the knowledge they get from it.

Benevolence

The essence of aikido is peace and benevolence, so it is quite difficult to keep a violent mind through the learning process. To the same extent that your ability grows, so do your calm and your aversion to violence. I also have the impression that those who develop this peacefulness seldom tempt others to attack them. Peacefulness is just as contagious as aggression – hopefully even more so.

When the Japanese converted their *jutsu* into *do*, this was one of their central ambitions. Out of the warrior skills of the Samurai, they wanted to extract a peaceful content. The reformed martial arts were to be ways toward a noble spirit and purity, far from their original purposes. To the Japanese minds involved in this reform, anything else would be abomination. Aggression is vulgar, and minds set on challenge are crude. Those who focus on true martial art can foster no such cravings. They seek peace, and shun violence.

Therefore, aikido as self-defense is not a method to leave a fight as the winner of it. That leads to wounds, which take time to heal – on both the winner and the loser. Aikido shall prevent fights from commencing at all, or put a gentle stop to fighting if an attack is already on the way.

Certainly, it seems like a utopian idea. It is. It can't be reached in a moment. But already long before it has developed to that point, aikido is milder as self-defense than many of its sibling arts, and that mildness actually increases its effectiveness. Not that this quality is what keeps people training aikido for decades.

The author doing kotegaeshi, a throwing technique, at a seminar in Pardubice, Czech Republic. Photo by Leos Matousek.

Delight

I have mentioned something about what attitude and methods are the most fruitful for making progress in aikido. But one question precedes it: Why learn aikido, at all? It is indeed a legitimate question. Those who don't have some kind of answer to it, no matter how deep down in their subconscious, are not likely to remain for very long in a dojo. We need a motif, if we are to pursue our training.

Aikido contains a number of arguments on several levels. The most immediate one is the good the exercises do to the body. You also improve the agility and skills of your limbs, straighten your posture, and increase your balance. Self-defense is another plausible gratification, although I have yet to meet an aikidoist who regards it as essential.

At the next level are the life-giving energy, *ki*, the pursuit of finding one's center, *tanden*, and other sweet Eastern secrets. But all of this might just as well be like pie in the sky when you die, a distant mirage, maybe just fake, if not the path to acquiring those benefits had its charm, too.

The way is the goal
I doubt that any of the great goals have solid value, without the delight one can feel during aikido training. The way is the goal. So, if the way is not enough of a reward, then the future is unlikely to have any more to offer. Aikido training should be fulfilling from the first moment on, in one way or other. Those who do not feel it should probably search for something else on which to spend their time.

Fulfillment is elusive. By its own nature, it is changing and inexplicable. Still, everyone can feel it, without a doubt. Either it is present or it is not. You need no master to tell you what is the case. If you don't feel it, then it just isn't there. The only ones who do not admit this are those who want to make themselves rulers over the lives of others. They claim to know what they cannot prove, and to understand what they cannot explain. They are bluffing.

Although it might take three years to realize your own and your teacher's potential, it does not mean that you have to wait as long to decide if you benefit from spending that time. The content can take time to grasp completely, but it only takes an instant to sense it. You feel immediately, deep inside, if there is something of value or not. So, you can at once decide if you should remain or move on.

This inner sense is the only trustworthy motivation. It is better to hold on to this sense, even if it leads to numerous interruptions and farewells, than to restrain oneself into slavery, supported only by some idea about self-discipline.

The same inner sense should be present in the training, too. Even if the training is strenuous, maybe occasionally painful, or dreadfully monotonous, this sense brings a feeling of delight. As long as you feel delight, you are on the right track.

The delight I refer to is quite different from pleasure, ambition, pride, or the prospect of benefit. Delight is humble and generous. It hides from those who look only for personal gain, but never deserts the benevolent. It is not only able to show an accessible path, since there are many to choose between. It shows the nicest path, the one that makes the very gods smile.

I believe that those who don't feel delight in their training are doing something wrong. But those who feel delight will discover that their training partners feel the same, and so do all those who surround them. No other motivation is necessary, and no other reward is worth chasing.

Aikitaiso, warm-up, at Brandbergen, Sweden. Photo by Gunilla Welin.

Aikido basics

Do – the way 道

The word aikido consists of three concepts that are all of them quite complex, to say the least: *ai*, *ki*, and *do*. The first one stands for harmony, or to unite. The second word is that of life energy. The third is way or path. Together, they are best understood if read backward: the way through life energy to harmony.

But that, too, is cryptic. One needs to pause at each word, and contemplate it separately. Again, we do well to use the backward order, starting with the word *do*, the way.

It helps to study the writing of the word closely. The word is written with *kanji*, by which the Japanese mean the complicated writing by pictures, originating in China.

The pictogram for *do* is a combination of two pictures. One is the symbolic picture of a head. The other part symbolizes a step, walking forward. So, the combination shows a head in forward advance. With a western expression: mental development. This suggests much more than the mere transport between point A and B. It is not just any road, although the sign can be used that profanely, as well. But *do* means more.

The pictogram symbolizing the head does so by combining the eye with eyebrows. Pointing out the eye as the most important part of the face is nothing unique to Eastern thinking. This is also done in western tradition, and confirmed by the psychology of perception, which has found that we trust our vision more than any other of our senses. What we see dominates how we perceive the world.

The sign for stepping forward or advancing consists of two parts. One is the symbol of the foot, and the other is what the great Sinologist Bernhard Karlgren referred to as an older form of the sign for man. Those two parts combined describe how a man weighs over on his foot, which is an elegant symbol of taking a step, since that is done by moving one's weight from one foot to the next, in order to advance the former. It is also interesting because it points out

The kanji do, the way. Ink calligraphy by the author.

the one of the feet that we would regard as the least important in taking a step – the one remaining, instead of the one
moving forward. But it stresses that one needs to be steady
on one's foot when advancing. Movement is dependent on
being grounded.

Combined, the sign for *do* has a lot to say. In his thinking, man can advance if he uses his eyes and is steady in his
stride. So, in two ways it focuses on reflection and careful
consideration. The eye inspects, and the foot weighs heavily
on the surface. Thereby, it is a way that is present on the
spot.

I want to liken it to the deer that halts almost in mid-
step, and examines its surroundings carefully, its muscles

ready for an immediate leap. Any second, it takes off in a certain direction, but until then it is frozen on the spot. Frozen, yet full of movement, like a film stopped in one of its frames.

Human beings, too, are sometimes halted in the middle of their rush through life, and wonder what is the best direction to continue. We might not need a preset goal, but we do need a direction in order to move at all, and to reach something through the span of our life. The way, described by the pictogram, is primarily the spiritual journey of man – toward completion, enlightenment, or whatever sublime goal we can fathom.

Taoism

For more than two thousand years, the way has been a central concept in the East. The pictogram is from China, where it is called *tao* (or *dao* in modern transcription), and it plays a big part in the oldest texts of Chinese philosophy. It has its most prominent role in *Tao Te Ching*, the Book on the Way and Virtue, which was composed several centuries BC. Its 81 verses about how to live one's life are said to have been written by Lao Tzu, and form the basis of Taoism.

In *Tao Te Ching*, the way is much more than man's course through life. It is the very order and ruling power of the universe. All parts of the universe, "the ten thousand things", follow the way naturally, like electrons circle the nucleus of an atom, and like water streams through a riverbed. The way is the great order of nature, and it existed already before the universe emerged. According to Lao Tzu, man has a free choice of either yielding to this life order, whereby fate will treat him well, or defy the order and unavoidably suffer because of it. A person who lives according to the way has virtue.

The way of Taoism is such a great thing that it becomes an almost indescribable mystery. It is above and beyond everything else – not like an ultimate god, but a principle that gods, too, have to obey. The first verse of *Tao Te Ching* reads:

The way that can be walked is not the eternal way
The name that can be named is not the eternal name
The nameless is the beginning of Heaven and Earth
The named is the mother of the ten thousand things
Therefore:
Free from desire you see the mystery
Filled of desire you see the manifestations
Those two spring from the same source
but differ in names
There's the secret
The secret of secrets
The gate to all mysteries

It is not a way that is easy to follow, either for deer or man. It is what it is, and we can only try to live up to it, through our virtue. If we relinquish our desires, we can sense its secret, and when we feel our desires, we see its manifestations. Maybe the perspectives meet at the extremes: When we are free from desires, and when we are filled with them, we see the same.

Zen

However, aikido is not as grand and cryptic as Taoism. Although Morihei Ueshiba was no Zen Buddhist, it makes sense to approach aikido through the Zen description of the way. The other martial arts use the same suffix: judo, kendo, iaido, karatedo, and so on. The same is true for budo, the general term for Japanese martial arts.

In Zen, the way is like a path along which one travels, but not really to reach a goal. There is kind of a goal in Zen: *satori*, which approximately means enlightenment. Still, there is not just one satori to be attained. There are several, and no fixed method to reach them. The person who experiences satori always does so in sudden surprise, and the only thing to do after it is to recommence with everything.

You reach your satori, that glimpse of absolute clarity, a moment when no mystery is beyond comprehension, and no circumstance in existence is complicated. This moment is ever so liberating and healing. The force gained and the inner calm found are used by taking on life even more wholeheartedly than before, and even more from the ground.

You recommence, and make everything more demanding. New satori will come in the future. It happens now and then, sometimes minutely, and sometimes in splendor, in aikido as well as in other spiritual pursuits. But as a goal to take aim at, satori is far too erratic. It comes and goes with the same suddenness. Such things cannot be aims. Actually, those who hunt satori moments of clarity are unable to reach them, because the effort blocks the mind.

Therefore, the way is the goal in Zen. You practice your art for hours, days, and years. The more you can desert the thought of what you might reach, the more can come your way. The real development happens in the hidden, behind what seems to take place, and within the development that you can yourself perceive. The big breakthrough is not a pot of gold at the end of the rainbow. It hides exactly at the spot where you stand – here and now.

The way of aikido can indeed seem monotonous. You just have to train, *keiko*, and continue to train, without fostering any ideas of what you will gain from it. That way, your own ambition and imagination are no limits to what you can accomplish. Still, the way has a definite direction. It infallibly leads toward the true and the natural – if you walk it without prerequisites.

Both in Zen and in the history of the martial arts, there are lots of anecdotes about the conditions of the way. They all teach that you can only remain on the way, and head in the correct direction, if you do it unconditionally. Reason is a bad guide. Speculation and analysis lead the wanderer astray. Aikido should be grasped intuitively. The movements should appear without plan, like reflexes.

In the beginning of the way, you copy your teacher to learn the elaborate techniques. But as soon as you have made them work and can repeat them effortlessly, you should forget about them. You stop copying. Instead you create the movements from inside of you. Thereby, every

Shomenate extension at a seminar in Plzen, Czech Republic. Photo by Antonín Knízek.

time you do the movements, they will come out softer, more natural, and truer. They will automatically develop toward perfection.

So, the way in aikido is walked with an empty head, and without a fixed destination. Without a plan, like a sleep-walker. Indifferent to the journey's progress, like one marching on the spot.

Ki – life energy   氣

All the way from India to the eastern end of Asia, breathing exercises of many different kinds are important parts of human self-curing. It is common knowledge among those peoples that breathing is the major key to health and well-being. Practicing breathing exercises daily, increases the chances of staying in shape.

It is odd that similar traditions have not emerged in the western world, although we have known since ancient times that breathing is the very prerequisite for life – from its starting point with the newborn baby's first scream to the dying man's last sigh. In between, western culture seems just to take breathing for granted, something to be carried out solely by the autonomous nervous system, as if such basic biological functions were unworthy of our attention.

Maybe it is a characteristic of our culture, for good or bad: We neglect the ordinary and natural, in order to devote ourselves to all the oddities we can come up with.

The square

Among the many Eastern breathing exercises there is one that works according to the principle of the square: four equal sides. You breathe in through the nose in an extended, deep inhalation all the way to the bottom of you abdomen. Then you hold your breath for just as long, followed by an equally long exhalation through your nose or your mouth. Finally you hold your breath for the same amount of time, before starting over again.

It is important to breathe deep and calmly. Shorter intervals than, say, six seconds, are not that meaningful. You should also make sure to have a good posture, with your back straight, your shoulders open, and your belly slightly protruding.

You don't need to repeat this breathing square very often for its result to appear: well-being, relaxation, and the air will sort of taste better.

Extending the intervals is good training and a natural development of this exercise. Then you will quickly become aware of its major difficulty: Three of the four sides of this square are easily prolonged, but it is shockingly difficult to hold your breath for any amount of time after an exhalation. The chest aches and the body releases all kinds of alarm signals.

So, you should set the length of the intervals to how long you can hold your breath after exhaling, without too

The kanji ki, life energy. Ink calligraphy by the author.

much discomfort. You should avoid having your torso cramp in an effort to resist breathing in. The exercise should lead to relaxation, not a battle between your conscious will and the instincts.

Extended breath
There is one way of extending the intervals quite a lot, and still feel calm. Instead of holding your breath by tightening your muscles, so to say putting the lid on it, you should

imagine that the inhalation or exhalation continues, although there is no air passing. When you have filled your lungs with air, you keep the feeling of inhaling, and when you have emptied them you remain in a feeling of exhaling.

It may seem odd, but it is nothing trickier for your fantasy than to imagine a movement before making it. Although the air is not flowing, you can feel a kind of buzz inside, a stream all through the body, from the bottom of your abdomen to your nostrils. Your breathing loses a beginning and an end. It just turns between in and out – and by time that difference, too, is evened out. Breathing becomes a steady flow, at the same time both in and out.

The sensation that is awakened and enforced by this exercise, this immaterial flow – that is *ki*, the cosmic life energy.

Oxygen

Ki works similar to breathing. It can be described as breathing inside the breathing, the proper life-giving essence of it – sort of like the hidden function of oxygen in the air. What happens when we breathe is that we pick up oxygen and leave carbon dioxide, in a constant, vital cycle. Oxygen hides in the air. Ki is also hidden, within and beyond the air we breathe.

The similarities between oxygen and ki are so striking that a modern analyst would probably like to explain ki as nothing but an old assumption in lack of knowledge of oxygen. Although the existence and function of oxygen were unknown, everyone could observe the necessity of breathing in order to stay alive. It made sense to suppose a hidden essence in the air, a life force that had to constantly flow through us, for us to stay alive.

Still, this is far from all that ki is in the Eastern perspective. Ki is not at all caught by the same boundaries as those of oxygen. For example, ki needs not follow the track of the air, through nose or mouth down to the lungs, in order for it to spread through the body like oxygen does. Ki can flow through us in any direction – in through the soles of the feet

Nobuyoshi Tamura, 8 dan Aikikai shihan, at a seminar in the author's dojo. Photo by Paul Ericsson.

or the palms of the hands, out through fingertips or forehead or chest. It moves completely independent of material laws.

Ki should rather be seen as all the senses formed into a beam of attention. If ki is a kind of ether, it consists of the very insight *I am*, the awareness of existing and relating to the outside world. If life equals movement, then ki is the will behind each movement, the impulse to it, and something that prepares for it. The body moves by muscles and bio-chemical combustion, but the will to move is fueled by ki. And the will precedes and rules the body.

Intention
Maybe we can call ki the ether of intention. Let's say you want to throw a snowball on a road sign. First you create in your mind a trajectory for your snowball to go from your hand to the road sign. Actually, this arc does not begin at the snowball in your hand, but inside your body, from where the force needed for the throw comes. That is the bottom of your abdomen, in your center, *tanden*, the core of your will-power.

The imagined trajectory of the snowball, which starts in the abdomen and ends on the road sign, is a flow of ki. The stronger this flow is, the more fixed the course of the snowball will be, and the more distinctly it will hit the target. All the movements in aikido are done with this spirit.

Flow

In Chinese, it is called *chi* (or *qi* with a modern transcription). The pictogram consists of two parts – one symbolizing a rice plant, the other steam. That is the boiling rice, the foremost symbol of life-supporting nutrition in the East. Rice is not edible until it has been boiled. Only when it has been given energy, can it give energy.

So is ki, as well. Movement is the prerequisite, and circulation is the condition. He who closes his faucets and locks his ki inside will shrivel. In him, the life force becomes stale, and he loses his spark. To increase your power, you must let ki flow out of you. This is another similarity to breathing – the one who does not exhale is equally unable to inhale. You must give to get, you must empty yourself to fill yourself, and you must throw away in order to win something new.

Life is change, movement without beginning or end, without any fixed starting point or final destination. Ki is the same.

Spirals

The flow of ki does not move in straight lines, but rather like heavenly bodies: in curves. Ki moves in spirals within spirals within spirals. The natural movement for ki is like the serpentine – the seemingly straight line is really a spiral shooting off. Within that spiral is another and another.

If you want to stimulate your flow of ki, you should choose rounded movements instead of straight ones, and returning courses instead of disappearing ones. The most natural thing for ki is to flow strongly in movements similar to those of heavenly bodies: ellipses.

In both layman astronomy and aikido, there is a lot of talk about circles. It is just as wrong in both. Natural aikido, flowing in the same orbits that ki is inclined to, forms ellipses. The same is true for planets and asteroids. Some planets, such as Neptune and Earth in our solar system, move in orbits that seem circular, but studied in detail they prove to be ellipses – with the sun in one of the focal points. Close to the sun they have their maximum velocity, and they move the slowest when they are the farthest away from it. No heavenly body has a steady speed. They accelerate and decelerate. That, too, is natural for aikido and for ki.

Constant speed and straight lines are unchangeable, like death. Since ki is the very energy of life, its form and expression are always the farthest from what likens death. Ki can expand or contract, accelerate or slow down, but never stand still.

The person who is able to harmonize completely with ki is able to direct it, but does so in ways that fit it, in orbits it strives for by itself. Then ki is not only a resource for man, but an unlimited flow through all of cosmos. You feel and follow this flow, like in a universal dance, like music of the spheres.

Universal
Morihei Ueshiba talked about ki as something personal and something universal. Each person's individual ki flow must strive toward joining with the universal flow. Just stimulating your ki to perform one or other feat is a petty ambition, worth little else than ridicule.

When ki flows without limit, it gives a spiritual experience that makes anything individual meaningless. You start to breathe the ether of the cosmos, and the *I am* that forms the core of your own ki merges with the being of the universe. You cease to be separate from existence, but become one with the world.

Ueshiba also talked about positive and negative ki. The latter is destructive, a force that separates itself from its surroundings and rarely does other than destroy. It suppresses, inhibits, and damages, leading closer to death. With a positive unselfish spirit you get ki that can create, cure, lead right, and go beyond the limitations of your ego.

Those who make their ki negative want to force it into straight lines, or stop it on the spot. They want to curb their

Kokyunage practice at the author's dojo Enighet in the mid-1990's. Jonas Dahlqvist, nowadays 4 dan Aikikai, is tori. Photo by Ulf Lundquist.

own ki, thereby also the ki of others. Such people can cause some trouble, and occasionally even impress others, but what they do never feels pleasant. Unfortunately, they can sometimes also transform the ki of others to the negative.

So, when you train your ki it is of utmost importance not to do it for your own sake, and not let yourself be trapped by the feats you can accomplish with it. You should give all you get, and let it flow for everyone's delight.

In western occult tradition there are similar warnings. They speak of white and black magic, where the former is benevolent and soft in its expression, while the latter is hard and destructive.

Probably these things can be equally well approached with the polarity of love and power. With ki as well as magic, it is quite possible to be attracted by the prospect of power, but that darkens it. You should throw away the ability you achieve, because it is worth nothing compared to the good spirit you can spread.

Psi

Western research into parapsychology talks about *psi* as a collective name for powers that are yet to be explained, such as telepathy, clairvoyance, telekinesis, and so on. If these phenomena are real, some kind of force or ability must lie behind it. For a deeper understanding, it makes sense to approach the Eastern concept of ki.

The parapsychology researchers have found another similarity to ki. In their experiments, they have found that they get the best results if the person examined is relaxed, trusting, and does not struggle to succeed.

In Asia, ki is so established that it contains a world of development and application. For example, traditional medicine and massage work mainly with the ki flow and how it runs through the patient's body. In massage, it is the ki of the masseur that stimulates the ki of the patient. The anatomical treatment is of lesser importance. In acupuncture the meridians, which are ki flow routes in the patient, are stimulated. Overall, ki is such a generally accepted concept in the East that it is rarely given the metaphysical connotation it always gets in western contemplation of it.

Another example of this is that in aikido, ki and the stimulation of its flow is not the main object of the training. It is an important part, certainly, but mostly in the same way that gasoline is needed for a car to move, and food and drink make man capable of action. Of course the quality of the fuel is important for the result – but it is not at all the same as the result. The interesting thing is what can be accomplished with ki. That is the great challenge.

Ai – harmony   合

The first syllable in the word aikido is the easiest of the three to draw in *kanji*, the pictogram, but far from as easy to translate. We usually say that *ai* (in Chinese *he*) means harmony, but that particular word is not used for it in any dictionary. It is more correct to translate it 'joining', 'agreement', or 'unity'. The word is also used in certain measurements.

The pictogram consists of a mouth, the number one, and the roof of a house. It can be interpreted as: under this roof, everybody speaks with one mouth. That is indeed an indication of unity.

In the combination of the word aikido, the most common translation of its first part is still harmony. It points out a unity that is not just the absence of conflict, but so fundamental that it has become like a state of its own, a peacefully working power.

To Morihei Ueshiba and his followers, aikido is not a way to victory in battle, nor solely a path away from battle itself. In spite of their obvious advantages, such things are basically just negations and therefore cannot last. The absence of something is never as vital as the abundance of something else.

The kanji ai, joining. Ink calligraphy by the author.

A world without war would be no lasting blessing, unless everyone could feel that peace is something of itself, something palpable, permeating civilization. Peace must be more than just the detente between two wars. Unity must be more than just the silence between two quarrels. Therefore the word harmony is preferred.

It indicates a sweet situation with such luminescence and attraction that nobody who has felt it will ever be inclined to break the calm. That is a unity more pleasant than any conflict can be exciting, and a peace that is sweeter than any war can be frightening. The good state of things must be so overwhelming that its counterpart pales and becomes petty in comparison. Only when gaining such a shine, *ai* becomes the most important of the three words in aikido. Only then, harmony becomes the finest reward of our training.

Like this

In Zen, riddles are often used to lead the student toward satori. These are called *koan*, and seem at first to be impossible paradoxes. The best known such koan is: What is the sound of clapping with one hand?

It has happened to me more than once, when I told

somebody this koan, that he actually started swinging one of his hands so that it made a clapping noise all by itself. The fingertips hit the palm of the hand. Some are quite good at it. Of course, their answer is correct. Even those who lack that agility can give a correct answer by simply swinging one hand in the air, like in an applause, and say: "Like this!"

The word *ai* in aikido is also kind of a koan, a paradoxical riddle that is almost impossible to solve with words alone. You have to do like with the hand clapping – show it in motion and action, and say: "Like this!" The great sweet harmony is no thesis that can be written down in books. It is ardent action, a solution in the moment and the exact situation.

In aikido, you never remain on the spot when an attack comes. You move to the side. If you walk on a railroad track and the train comes, you step off from the track. Anything else would be devastating. That is as evident as the clapping of hands. Why collide? Why stand in the way of a force that shows its direction so clearly? Ai is to always step off the railroad track, and never to halt or challenge – even if you have the power to do so. Also the little train of a model railroad is allowed to pass. You don't step off the track because you are unable to stop the train, but because you do not want to stop it. The harmony of aikido is to gladly allow the train to pass, and watch it disappear in the distance. There you stand, waving.

This might at first sound like a principle of passivity, a way to avoid damage by surrendering to anything. That is not the case. You halt no movement and do not go against any force – nor do you give up or give in to them. You avoid the conflict in such a way that conflicting is not successful. Using the analogy of the train again: If the train's purpose were to ram the person on the railroad track, that intention became null and void. No collision, nobody subdued. When the train disappears, you step back onto the track and continue just like before.

Berlin based Mikael Eriksson at a seminar in the author's dojo, joining with Jonas Dahlqvist. Photo by Anders Heinonen.

Love

Most of the misery in the world seems to stem from conflicting wills. One person wants what another does not want to give away, or one wants to stand on a space occupied by another, and so on. But the world is big and rich enough for all. We should be able to live full and pleasant lives, without robbing others.

This is the conviction of aikido. Harmony is the highest natural state, so anyone opposing it must fail. The one who is willing to do battle for his own gain will neither succeed with his ambition nor find a battle at all. When he wants to push another person aside he will just be led back to his own place. When he tries to drag others along they will escape, so that he just stumbles ahead on his own. His force strikes right back at him, and each time he is returned to where he started.

If aikido did not work exactly like that, it would encourage battle and hostility instead of leading to their disappearance. The harmony that does not incorporate all, will sooner or later prove to incorporate none.

Those who seek battle are in a state of confusion, of misunderstanding, but they can be corrected neither by being subdued nor by having their wishes come true. The harmony of aikido shall be so pleasant that it seduces them to the right course, and so evident that it opens their eyes. Then peace is not just time spent in nervous anticipation of the next war, but a majesty that no one is tempted to revolt against, and no aggressor has the power to defeat.

To Morihei Ueshiba, this grand harmony was so central and so sweet that the older he got, the more he compared this concept to one pronounced the same in the Japanese language: *Ai* written with another pictogram means love. Harmony in aikido should be so universal and fervent that it transforms into love.

Triangle, circle, and square

A recurring symbol for aikido is the combination of these three geometric figures: the triangle, the circle, and the square. They can be explained on several levels. On one level they are images of how aikido should be practiced, and on another they are linked to Eastern philosophy.

The triangle represents the basic position *hanmigamae*, where the directions of the feet and the angle of the body suggest a triangular shape. Even more so, the triangle shows how to meet the attacker – with a step forward and to the side. If the attacker is the base of the triangle, the entering step is one of its sides. One should not move toward the attacking force, but to the side of it.

The circle shows how the aikido techniques should be done – in curves around both the attacker's and one's own center. As Osensei said: every circle has a center. The circle is a symbol of the circular movements of aikido, and of the body's center, which has to be in the middle of every move. Maybe the ellipse would be an even more suitable symbol. It has a more extended curve than the circle, as do the aikido

Ukemi, fall, at Brandbergen dojo.

movements, and it has two focal points, two centers – like that of oneself and one's aikido partner.

The square stands for determination and control, like in the pinning that most aikido techniques finish with, or the throw that sends the attacker in another direction than he or she expected to go. The square is the heavy stability one gets from focusing on one's center.

Also, it is with the principle of the square that one establishes contact with the partner. Both the triangle and the circle are evasive by nature, but with the square a meeting takes place. Without it, aikido would be like a passing gust of air, a mist that certainly would make every attack futile, but it would not cause any development.

Unity

Morihei Ueshiba talked about the three symbols united into one, like drawing them one within the other: the triangle inside the circle, inside the square. This unity is essential in making all three aspects join in an aikido technique. They have to cooperate, so they have to be in balance.

If you concentrate too much on the triangle, and neglect

the other two, your aikido will be sharp but fragile. If you focus on the circle, your aikido will be swirling but indecisive. If you focus on the square, your aikido will be strong but hard.

It is not only in aikido that those three geometrical figures have become meaningful symbols. You find them in Zen as well, in Taoism, and in many other doctrines. For example, the circle is often a symbol of the all – or nothing. The square symbolizes the worldly things, like the bricks of walls. The triangle often represents divine principles, such as in the trinity of Christianity.

Tanden – the center   丹田

Not only at first glance, aikido techniques are like labyrinths. Arms go here and legs go there, hands are held at odd angles, and the body is turned this way or that. How to direct one's body into the right movements seems as impossible to solve as the trickiest *koan*. And then you have to guide another person into the same patterns, or several attackers at once. It is easy to shake one's head and surrender in front of such complications. This must be too much to keep on one's mind?

Yes it is. If man were a kind of machine that had to be programmed and calibrated for each ability to stick, then aikido would quickly become too much to handle. But man is no machine, and aikido is not a random pattern of tricky movements. Aikido is to be natural, and man is since birth deeply rooted in the natural.

You only need to be receptive to your inner voice, your inner certainty, to immediately manage the aikido movements as easily as if you had invented them. If you cannot feel this instinct for what is right, if this inner compass does not give a reading during the aikido training – then you are

on the wrong track to begin with, and no effort in the world can compensate for it.

The red rice field

Man's root in the natural, his inner compass and infallible sensory organ, is his center. In Japanese it is called *tanden* (in Chinese *dantian*). It is situated in the middle of the body, at the lower abdomen, about three finger widths down from the navel. The same point is also the body's center of mass.

In Indian tradition the body has seven main *chakra*, points of power, from the pelvis up to the top of the head. Chakra really means wheel, implying its active role, and each of the chakra has its own characteristics. Tanden is the same as the second chakra from the bottom, with the Indian name *svadhisthana*.

The pictogram for *tanden* has two parts. The upper one means cinnabar red, and the lower is the symbol for a rice field. So: the red rice field. Since rice is the primary nutrition in this part of the world, it does in itself represent life energy. A whole field is life energy in abundance, and if it is glowing red – like the shimmering red cinnabar crystal – then this expresses a formidable level of life energy.

The center of this force is a point a few centimeters below the

The kanji tanden, center. Ink calligraphy by the author.

navel, in the middle of the body. This point is also called *ki kai tanden*, an ocean of ki in this cinnabar red rice field, or *seika no itten*, which means the only point. In English, we can simply refer to it as the center.

To the beginner, this center is as hard to imagine, as it is to perceive. Therefore it is of utmost importance that the aikido students try to stimulate their ki and the perception of their center from the very beginning. The two lead to one another. Ki exercises make you aware of your center, the source of ki inside you, and when you become aware of your center, ki will flow from it.

Tanden is the ocean of ki, the endless source of life energy, and also the point that ki will flow to and from. The more you focus on your ki, the clearer your perception of your center will be, and the more you focus on your center, the stronger the ki flow will become.

To the center
In aikido, the center is the starting point for your balance and stability, being your body's center of mass. Also, it is the source through which most of your ki will flow. When you concentrate on your center you become steady. Your movements become powerful and confident, and they spread a flow of ki from within. Of course, these things increase by time. All the movements in aikido begin in the center, and return there through elliptic and spiral paths.

This is the most obvious in the sword cut.

Katana, the Japanese sword, is grabbed by both hands. In the basic position you hold the sword at the distance of one fist from your body, in front of your center. The tip of the sword points toward the opponent's eyes (the left eye, to be precise). The angle of the sword is not that steep, since the blade has its curve, and the opponent is at a bigger distance than in unarmed training. You raise the sword by pushing it forward from your center, so that it moves upward in a semi-circle. You cut by pulling it back the same way, to your center. You inhale to your center in the draw, and you exhale from your center in the cut.

Mokuso, also called zazen, seated meditation, before the start of an aikido class at a seminar in Plzen, Czech Republic. Photo by Antonín Knízek.

Although it is rarely as evident as with the sword cut, all movements in aikido have the same course of events: out from the center, and back to it. If you lose this link to your center in the movements, the technique becomes weak and fragile, often failing. Tanden is like a guiding rule, a constantly present key to the aikido techniques.

Later on, tanden becomes much more than that.

I am

I have heard that in psychiatry they talk about getting centered, about recovering one's center. What they refer to is the feeling of being lost, which we can easily be overcome by. Existence is much vaster and much more complicated than we are at all times able to handle.

People stuck in confusion lose the sense of rooting and stability that would give them the capacity to recover after emotional turmoil. They need to learn how to sit down within themselves, how to peel away the entire mental muddle until they uncover a pure and lasting sense of who they fundamentally are. We need to shake off all distractions, to find that we remain what we are – through emotional turmoil and the whipping winds of change.

In Eastern thought, the human center is about the same. In the very core of my being, there is no doubt: I am, and I remain through all adventures and revolutions. Contrary to psychiatry, though, this center is not only mental therapy or concentration exercises. Tanden is very concrete, indeed. It is a core in the lower abdomen, as tangible as the heart that beats in one's chest. In traditional Eastern thought this center is quite real.

Look at small children who have just learned how to walk. Their bellies protrude like on sumo wrestlers, and they take their steps just as heavily, with just as much concentration in the center. Unfortunately, it is not rare that they lose contact with their center when they grow up. The immediate effect is a loss of balance and weakness in the movements, but what may follow is an increasing confusion of the senses. Sadly, lots of people live their whole lives like that.

If you exercise sensing your center in the lower abdomen, and use it for support whatever you do, then a certainty about your own essence will grow. You regain contact with yourself. You find comfort in knowing that you exist, and increasingly realize who you are. The way to self-realization goes through tanden.

In aikido training you should always concentrate on your center, so that it more and more becomes the initiator and motor of the movements. This physical exercising of tanden also has a mental counterpart. The more familiar you get with your center in training, the more you also feel a center of your senses. You get rooted in existence and there is a decreasing risk of losing your physical or mental balance.

It is through your center that you become whole, and gain confidence independent of success or conquest. Therefore you are not shaken by adversity or defeat. This self-esteem is nothing but the straight and simple statement: I am what I am.

If I have to choose one element in aikido as the most important one, then without a doubt that would have to be tanden, the inner center of man. There is nothing more important in all of aikido. So, what essentially happens in aikido training is that two tanden interact, and are led through aikido principles to harmonious expressions.

Therefore, the most important task for all who train is to stimulate each other's center, help each other find and experience one's center, and then increasingly be able to express it.

Aiki – rhythm and direction

One story from old Japan tells about an ageing samurai who could feel that his time was up. Therefore, he wanted one last time to scrutinize his three sons as to their maturity and skills in *bushido*, the way of the warrior.

Above the sliding door to his room, he placed a little pillow so that it would fall when the door opened. Then he called his youngest son. When the son entered the room, the pillow fell and hit him on the shoulder. But before it landed on the floor, the youngster had drawn his sword and with a fierce cry cut it in half.

"Shame on you!" the father exclaimed, and continued with a sharp voice: "My son, you have understood nothing about bushido. You must practice much more."

After additional reprimands and advice on how to pursue his training of the samurai arts, the father sent his son away and put a new pillow above the door. He called the middle son.

This time too, the pillow fell, but before it hit the young man he had taken a quick step to the side, drawn his sword and cut it in half.

"My son," the father said with a solemn voice, "you practice our art diligently, but it is not enough. You still have a lot to learn, and must practice more."

Tachidori, defense against sword. The author shows the initial taisabaki step to avoid the attack, at a seminar in Pardubice, Czech Republic. Photo by Leos Matousek.

As soon as the son had left him, the father did the same thing with a third pillow, and called his oldest son.

The young man was just about to open the door to his father's room, but halted. Instead, his hand snuck up and carefully grabbed the pillow, before it had moved at all from its unstable position. Then he opened the door, stepped in, and returned the pillow to its place.

"My son, my son, you have indeed learned the way of the warrior! I can say with pride that you don't need me anymore," the father said and smiled wholeheartedly. "I ask you to look out for your brothers, and guide them on their continued pursuit."

Two-beat

One of Morihei Ueshiba's most important sources in creating aikido was the old martial art *Daito ryu Aikijutsu*. The word *jutsu* means technique, art, or skill, which stresses the practical and functional side of the martial arts. Aikijutsu is a strategy for winning in close combat, trained by samurai for centuries. In Japan there are hundreds of different jutsu, which have been passed on through many generations in samurai families. These arts were trained severely, and mostly kept secret within the families of their origin.

In this context, *aiki* is not really the mark of a spiritual path, but a practical course of action in combat, in order to ascertain victory. You unite your *ki* with that of the attacker, so that you can defeat him or her. Although this goal is meager, compared to what aikido can give, the strategy of this traditional application of aiki is still brilliant.

Basically, it is a question of rhythm:

Self-defense usually happens in sort of a two-beat. First, the attacking technique is blocked or parried, and then there is a counterattack. One, two. The problem with this is that the opponent has a good chance of blocking the counterattack, and then attack anew. If the combatants are of equal skill, this may go on for quite a while – like a game of tennis. There is no way of making sure to win the ball played. In the martial arts, where losing one "ball" is fatal, these odds are not good enough.

One might try to increase one's chances by quickening the counterattack as much as ever possible. The regular two-beat is replaced by the speedy double beat on a drum: ta-dum. If it is done skillfully, the opponent is unlikely to be able to defend himself. He is helplessly exposed, just by having attacked. So, already with this thinking, attacking is the worst kind of defense.

This rhythm is the most common in all the Eastern martial arts. They developed blocks and parries that would make the fastest counterattacks possible. Ta-dum.

Be one
It is still not enough – and it is not aiki, the blending of the energies of the combatants. For that to take place, everything must happen at once, at the first beat. Aiki is both fighters acting in unison. The samurai, with their razor sharp swords, could not trust anything else.

There is one simple exercise with sword against sword, which Morihei Ueshiba repeated all his life. The two swordsmen both make a cut toward each other's head at exactly the same time – but where one of them advances straight forward, the other moves forward to the side. The former will miss his target, but the latter not. Instead of colliding with the other, he moves away and strikes him slightly from the side.

Like most things in this book, this is easier to describe than to do correctly. The difficulty is mainly in what we usually call timing. You must draw for your cut at the same time as the opponent does, and you must slide to the side at the moment when the opponent is no longer able to redirect his strike.

This cannot be accomplished by tense readiness, where you try to react as soon as you see the opponent begin to charge. On the contrary, this needs relaxation and a special kind of sensitivity. You must forget yourself in order to tune in to your opponent, so that you react in almost the same way to the impulse of his will as his own muscles do. You must be one with your partner, and be at rest in his center. Then, when he gives himself the impulse to charge, he will automatically give you the impulse to avoid it. Your movement is synchronous with that of the attacker.

This is achieved through relaxation, through awaiting the attack without preconditions.

The winning step is possible for one simple reason: The one being attacked always knows what the attacker aims for. An attack is limited by the fact that it has a specific direction – toward the one being attacked. In aiki, this knowledge is quite sufficient to ensure success.

You do not need to figure out exactly what kind of attack will come, or how hard or strong it will be. You step out of the way, and already before that step you know where the attacker must be at the end of the attack. Since you know from where he comes and what he charges at, you can tell where he will be after the attack, and you can aim at that point instead of the position he started from. So, when both the cuts are done simultaneously, one will miss and one will not.

Aikido

Joint intention

Those are the fundamentals of aiki: It happens at the first beat, and the evasive movement makes the attacker miss, while the defender does not.

The sweet lesson in this strategy is that the attacker is vulnerable precisely because of his choice to attack. If he were instead to await the opponent's move, he would also be able to use the great advantage of aiki. Only the one attacking is vulnerable to aiki. So, the best is never to attack. Therefore, aiki is not only the cleverest of strategies, but the most ethical as well.

But if aiki stays on the level of these strategic features, aikido becomes little more than a system of self-defense, although a sophisticated one. There will still be a winner and a loser, which inevitably leads to new controversy.

The initiation of an attack can be described as a direction given to the ether of intention, called *ki*. That direction is also the one of the following actual attack. The flow of intention is the true substance of the attack, while the body movement and attack technique following are secondary – in time as well as in importance. If the intention is defied and interrupted, if the flow is hindered, then the conflict must remain. That is true also if the attacker is completely defeated.

Aiki is instead that the defender allows his ki, his intention, to join that of the attacker, as if for a common goal. Their ki shall have the same direction, and flow alongside one another like playmates, to a natural end for the movement that gets its character and form out of this joining. Mild and elegant techniques appear naturally in the moment when the attacker's and the defender's intentions go in the same direction. Therefore, you should always make sure that the aikido technique moves with the attacking force, instead of against it – all through the technique.

Kiai – gathering power 氣合

There was a market in the town square, and in addition to all the stands and salesmen was another kind of attraction. A little guenon monkey was chained to a pole, and anyone who wanted to test his skills could throw a spear at it. The chain was long enough for the monkey to run around the pole freely. Every time someone threw the spear, the guenon quickly snuck around to the backside of the pole, escaping the spear. It did not matter how fast the spear was thrown, or how long the thrower waited before doing it – the monkey was always on the backside of the pole before the spear hit it.

An increasing number of people gathered to admire the monkey's speed, and laugh at the failure of one confident man after another. Hours passed, and the monkey remained unharmed. One of the many men who tried was a young student of the famous *yari* master Jubei Taneda, but he failed as miserably as all the others.

He told his teacher about the test, and next day Taneda followed him to the market place. The imposing samurai lifted the spear and fixed his eyes on the monkey. Suddenly, it became paralyzed, made a short scream, and fell to the ground, although Taneda had not even thrown the spear.

The samurai had used a silent *kiai*, and with such force that it had stunned the monkey.

Not the shout
Kiai exists in all budo. Mostly, it is expressed by sound – a forceful shout at the moment the technique is done. Still, kiai is not the actual shout, but a gathering of power of which the shout is a sign. So, a soundless kiai is also a kiai, although more difficult to master.

The two words that kiai consists of are the same as in aiki. The reverse order is essential. It shows another purpose, another direction. In aiki it is *ki*, the life energy, which shall lead to harmony, but in kiai it is instead harmony that shall

Morihiro Saito (1928-2002), 9 dan Aikikai shihan, showing jo technique at Iwama, Japan, with Swedish instructor Ulf Evenås, 7 dan shihan. Photo by Jöran Fagerlund.

lead to ki. Kiai is to gather one's ki for one direction, one aim. You focus completely on what is to be done, and let all your inner resources join to reach this goal. Kiai is to raise all your power and ability in one moment, and one movement.

All your ki flows into one stream, like when the ruby in a laser shapes the light into one sharp beam. Just as with the laser beam, such a concentration of ki can have an overwhelming effect, according to the Eastern tradition. Your movement becomes irresistible, your intent and technique become so sharp that success is certain already before anything has happened.

It is not unknown in the western world. The weightlifter shouts when he struggles with the biggest weights. The wrestler shouts when he throws his opponent. The shout is a well-known method to gain extra force, to stand pain, or to make other people halt in anticipation. Mark Twain joked about this when he said that his proud ancestors always walked into battle singing, in the last line, and ran out of it screaming, from the first line.

Well, this shout is the outer sign of gathering power and letting it flow. Without the shout, insufficient breathing might halt this flow and diminish the power. When you really need all your force, it is natural to open your mouth and let a sound out. In budo, this sound is exercised so that it comes voluntarily, and helps the release of additional inner powers.

We know from medical science that adrenaline is the body's method of mobilizing all that it is able. Kiai becomes a technique to stimulate the adrenaline, and immediately raise the personal resources beyond what they normally manage.

The shout shall come all the way from the bottom of the abdomen, from the ocean of ki, and be much more than a mere sound. Volume is not the primary thing. If you strain yourself too much to make an animalistic roar, the power will clog up in your throat, and not find its way to the movement it was intended for. The sound is nothing but an unintentional result of the gathering of power, and not the other way around. A mere side effect. So, when you train the kiai, it is not a training in making the sound, but in gathering the power. You train your ability to instantly mobilize your energy and let it out.

Kiai becomes a self-clearing, cleansing exercise. When you have extended all your ki in one single moment and movement, you become like empty. Internal knots are untied, distractions lose their grip on the senses, and you stand alert, ready to take on whatever you set your mind to.

Three moments
It can be said that there are three different moments when kiai can be applied, with three separate purposes: before the movement, during the movement, and at the end of the movement.

Kiai before the movement, such as the silent one the samurai used instead of throwing his spear at the monkey, is partly to raise and cleanse one's own mind, and partly to shake the opponent out of balance. It is an imposing way of declaring: "Here I am!" It gives you pride and ability, to the same extent that the opponent is intimidated.

Kiai during the movement maximizes its power and precision, so that it completes its purpose without wavering or being warded off by the opponent. The feeling in this kiai should be irrevocable and inevitable. With such conviction in your voice, it becomes difficult for the opponent to escape your technique.

At the end of a movement, kiai is a way of marking completion, by being an explosion of power and concentration in that final moment. Such a kiai washes away any doubt that the battle is over. What was intended has been realized and cannot be undone. It is like when decision and action become one.

In karatedo, the third kiai is often used, for example when the bare hand hits an object. The kiai strengthens and protects the hand. Kendo, Japanese fencing, has a kiai that runs through all three moments, from the charge and far past the strike. That works as a kind of underlining of the technique and the unavoidable character of its whole course of events, as well as a lingering note stating – in a victorious call – that the battle now is over.

In aikido, silence is the most common, but when there is kiai, it is always at the time of the movement. Of course, silence does not necessarily mean that there is no kiai. It is often soundless, since aikido only tries to follow the force of the attacker. So the kiai in aikido should be one with the kiai of the attacker.

For that reason it is unthinkable in aikido to pierce the poor monkey.

Meaningful sounds

Morihei Ueshiba made sounds almost all the time, when he practiced aikido. All his techniques were accompanied by shouts and different sounds. Those were certainly kiai, but they also had another content. Ueshiba was deeply engaged

Kazuo Igarashi, 7 dan Aikikai shihan, showing kokyunage, a throwing technique, at a seminar in Stockholm. Photo by Magnus Hartman.

Peter Spangfort, 5 dan Aikikai and 3 dan Ki no Kenkyukai, doing kokyunage on tachidori, a sword attack. Photo by Binge Eliasson.

in *kototama*, the Shinto tradition of linking sounds to certain higher meanings. So, his kiai was both a way of gathering power, and a method to express a specific intention, uniting with a higher reality.

As you become familiar with the use of kiai, there is a natural tendency that the sounds get their characteristics from what was intended with them, and the attitude behind them. The attacker's kiai sounds differently from that of the defender, and kiai will also differ according to what technique is done. This is the most obvious in kendo, where the practitioners simply use the name of the target as their kiai for the corresponding movement. Strikes to the head are called *men*, referring to the head and helmet. Strikes to the wrist are called *kote*, which is wrist in Japanese, and strikes to the breast cuirass are called *do*.

In a similar direction the explanation might be found for a common kiai in karatedo, where students shout:

"Kiai!"

Kiai also tends to become personal, whatever the purpose of it. People who have trained budo for some time usually develop sounds in their kiai that are individual preferences, rather than indications of what is intended with them. On the other hand, such a personal choice surely says something about what the practitioner wants his or her budo to be. An individual kiai reveals what that person wishes to express and achieve with his or her martial art. So, one should listen to one's own kiai and contemplate it.

Kamae – the perfect guard 構

Once, there was an old master of *chado*, tea ceremony, the pleasant art of making and serving tea. He was highly skilled at his art and a pride to his lord, one of the daimyo of Japan. When it was time for the daimyo to visit and show his respect to *shogun*, the ruler of Japan, he wanted to bring the tea master with him.

It was necessary to dress like a samurai for this journey. The tea master knew nothing about the sword art and samurai custom, but his daimyo insisted. So, he had to stick two swords inside his belt, although this was reserved for the samurai, and they went off to Edo (present Tokyo).

The shogun was amazed by the beauty of the master's tea ceremony, and his daimyo was very pleased. But one day, when the master walked the streets of Edo, he met a *ronin*, a samurai without a lord, who immediately challenged him to a duel. It was customary among the samurai to try out their skills on each other. For the sake of his daimyo's honor, the tea master could not refuse, nor could he confess that he was not a samurai. Instead, he asked his challenger for a delay of a few hours, in order to inform his daimyo and settle his affairs. This was granted.

The tea master hurried to visit the foremost fencing master of the city, and explained his situation.

"I know that I cannot win the duel," he said, "but for the sake of my lord it is necessary that I die like a samurai. Therefore, would you be so kind as to show me how to behave, so that my challenger does not suspect the truth?"

The fencing master was deeply moved by the humble request, so far from the fierce behavior of his fencing students.

"I will help you," he replied, "if you do the tea ceremony with me."

This was done, and the fencing master was just as amazed as the shogun had been.

"You need to know only one thing," the fencing master explained after the tea ceremony. "When you face your challenger, draw your sword and then think exactly as you do in your tea ceremony."

This instruction puzzled the tea master, but he went to meet the ronin and did what he had been told. He drew his sword and concentrated in exactly the same way as when performing the tea ceremony. The challenger also drew his sword, and approached his opponent cautiously.

No matter how the ronin searched, he found no open-

Chudankamae, middle level guard, with bokken against bokken, at a seminar in Lucenec, Slovakia. Photo by Martin Svihla.

ing in the tea master's guard. There was not a hint of a weak spot, on which to aim in a charge.

To attack a swordsman without any opening in his guard would be certain death. Therefore, after trying his opponent for a long time, the ronin had to surrender and lower his sword.

"I apologize," he said humbly. "I see that I cannot defeat you."

And he left.

Only kamae

In the budo arts, the basic guard position is called *kamae*. It is not the same for kendo, judo, karatedo, aikido, and the other arts, but the principles are the same. You should be ready, relaxed, and with an empty mind.

The *kanji* pictogram for the word is a little odd. It consists of the sign for wood or a tree, and the sign for a trellis and similar devices. This gives the impression of the guard posture as a complex construction, where each part has its specific place and function, and the solidity of the whole depends on the parts having found their correct positions.

Many people believe that the best defense is tense readiness, and to fill one's head with a great number of techniques and tricks to choose from when the attack comes. But such an attitude is easily deceived and lead astray. The brain is slower than the hand, and should not slow it down. The best kamae is to empty oneself of plans, worries, and the lust for victory, so that the reflexes are free to handle the defense. With such an attitude you cannot be taken by surprise.

When the tea master thought about his art he became empty and clear inside, like in deep rest. Therefore, no opening was visible in his guard. Although the tea master had no knowledge of the sword arts, the challenger was not misled. In this state of mind, the tea master would probably have responded correctly if attacked, although he had never handled a sword before.

Kamae is a sublime test of mastery. Already there, before any movement has commenced, the beginner is separated from the one with experience. There are countless stories from old Japan about how duels between samurai were decided already at kamae, without any sword strike. The one with superior kamae does not lose the battle.

One of the greatest Japanese swordsmen of present days was Kiyoshi Nakakura, who died in his 90th year, 2000. He had the grade 9th dan *hanshi* in both kendo and iaido (10th dan in those arts can only be given posthumously). He also practiced some aikido in his younger years. Once he told me how he examined kendo and iaido practitioners for dan grades. He only studied their kamae. Then he knew what grade to give them, and did not care about what they were doing during the rest of the examination.

Now and then he hesitated – should this practitioner have this or that dan grade? In those few cases he looked out for the very first movement. Whether this was a charge or a parry, Nakakura could immediately decide on the grade, and he closed his eyes. He never needed to see more.

No guard

As said above, kamae differs between the budo arts. This has to do with their techniques and purposes.

In judo you stand with your feet right below your shoulders, none in front of the other. This is the best starting position for the many judo throws and sweeps, if you want to be able to shift quickly between attack and defense. In the basic guard of karatedo you take a big step forward with one foot, so that your body is lowered, the back leg is stretched, and the front leg is bent. The feet are outside the line of the shoulders. This position is to give maximum stability and force to the dynamic karate techniques. In kendo you take about half a step forward, usually with your right leg, and lift both the heels from the floor so that you stand mainly on your toes. The feet are almost on the same line, well inside the span of the shoulders. This is to become a small target for the opponent's *shinai*, the fencing sword, and to be able to leap forward very quickly.

The most common basic guard in aikido, *hanmigamae*, is

a bit more extended than the half step of kendo. The back foot points to the side, the front foot points forward, and the body is turned slightly to the side – sort of like you are heading in two directions at once. This is also one of the reasons for it. You want support for movements to the side, as well as forward. The first movement is almost always the *taisabaki* step forward to the side. The back foot's side angle also gives the leg additional strength for a quick leap forward.

But the superior guard for aikido is that of no guard. Let us call it anti-kamae. In aikido you never accept the battle, and do not enter into it at all. For that reason there should be no guard that is preparation for battle. Truly harmonious aikido begins from the steps of ordinary walking, so that it is not even interrupted by carrying out the technique. Then kamae is nothing but the position you happen to be at when you halt your step: one foot a bit in front of the other, the body directed straight forward, and the hands hanging relaxed by your sides.

It is usually called *shizentai*, the natural or spontaneous posture. Morihei Ueshiba said that there is no specific guard position in aikido. The stances and movements are completely natural.

So, the optimal aikido kamae differs from those of all the other budo arts. It becomes invisible, non-existent. Therefore it has no weaknesses. It does not warn the attacker by showing readiness and ability, nor does it limit the options of the aikidoist by fitting one or other specific defense. It shall be nothing other than what it happens to be at the moment.

When in your basic posture you show no vigilance, you create no suspicion. When you do not signal the intention to defend yourself, others will not be tempted to challenge you. You become like air, eventually as vacuum.

Aggression needs a target. The more obvious the target is, the more aggression it will trigger. That is the same with animals and people. The instinct to attack is immediately awakened by seeing somebody flee or prepare to resist. Only the one who seems to perceive no threat at all can make the attacker forget his intention, or never get the idea to attack at all.

Trigger
In the aikido techniques, kamae is also used in quite a paradoxical way: to trigger the attack. By showing an opening in your kamae, you make your partner attack that exact point at the moment you show it. You open your guard, and thereby lure your partner to attack.

With persistent training you can in this way learn to maneuver and manipulate the attacker as invisibly as it is far-reaching – and decisive. Not even the most ferocious swordsman will run right into his opponent's guard, but if he perceives the slightest crack in that guard, a slight lack of concentration, then he will immediately charge. A defender who chooses to show such an opening can make the attacker go for it.

This is used in aikido. In your training, you should always tempt your partner to make the attack on which you want to practice the defense – so that the attack will be credible and executable, and also so that you can practice the art of secretly maneuvering the attacker.

If you choose instead to keep an impregnable kamae, or the anti-kamae that makes the opponent forget his will to attack – then there will not be much training. You will both just stand there. It might be ideal as self-defense, but quite boring at length in a dojo.

Kokyu – belly breathing   呼吸

Kokyu is written with two signs: *ko*, which means exhaling, and *kyu*, inhaling. Together they simply stand for breathing. In aikido, though, the word refers to the special abdominal breathing that is used to give power and stamina. You

Seiichi Sugano, 8 dan Aikikai shihan, showing kokyuho at a Stockholm seminar in the 1980's. Photo by Magnus Hartman.

should breathe with *tanden*, your center in the lower abdomen. This also stimulates your ki flow.

Maybe this is implied by the order of the two components in the word: You breathe out before you breathe in, but then what is there to breathe out? Ki, of course – the life energy that is not dependent on the lungs. It fills us already before we have taken our very first breath.

In western meaning, kokyu is to breathe with the diaphragm, the sheet of muscle between the chest and the abdomen. This is what opera singers, among others, are taught to do, so that they can sing loudly and keep a tone for long on a single exhalation. But in budo one should not focus on the diaphragm, although strictly physiologically speaking it is doing the job.

Instead, you should focus exactly on the body center, tanden, and your breathing should feel like a pair of bellows of that center. The breathing goes into your center and out from it, in an escalating flow that soon loses the difference between in and out. Breathing breaks free of the basic linear in and out, becoming a spiral movement where it is no longer possible to clearly distinguish between inhalation and exhalation.

That is shown by how the belly moves: not at all.

Good belly breathing demands a straight posture, where the belly should be allowed to protrude rather than being held in, no matter what modern beauty ideals may have to say about it. A significant such posture is seen on the Japanese sumo wrestlers – and on toddlers who are just learning to walk. When you breathe with a correct posture, your belly does not expand and contract significantly, but holds its form. Nor are she shoulders going up and down. Although kokyu is deep and powerful breathing, it becomes almost invisible.

Budo breathing

The invisible breathing is a clear advantage in budo training. It has been known for ages in the Japanese martial arts that man is the easiest to defeat when he is inhaling. That is when the body is the most fragile and weak, and the movements are the slowest. The attacker is wise to charge exactly when the opponent is inhaling. So, if the difference between breathing in and out is dissolved, and the body does not signal the shift from the one to the other, the attacker will have a hard time finding a moment for striking.

The aikido techniques show this process. In the beginning of learning them, you should make a big difference between inhaling and exhaling, where some phases of the technique are done during the former, and some during the latter. By time these differences diminish, so that the techniques become uninterrupted ellipses and spirals, where the direction of your breathing ceases to matter.

The basic cut with *katana*, the Japanese sword, shows this clearly. You grab the sword with both hands and hold it in front of *tanden*, your center. The position is called *chudan-kamae*, the middle guard, and it is the basic guard of the sword arts. Then you lift the sword over your head at the same time as you inhale, and cut forcefully forward and down, while you exhale. The sword stops at the chudan-kamae it started from.

The more you learn to master the sword, the less of a difference you will feel in this up and down of the sword, this in and out of the breathing. Finally, the whole movement becomes like a closed circle, with neither beginning nor end. Such a cut is difficult to escape.

The basic sword cut is one of the very best ways to exercise your belly breathing, as well as your center.

There are many aikido techniques that are just as obvious examples of belly breathing. They are named accordingly: *kokyuho*, which simply means breathing technique or breath control, and *kokyunage*, the breath throw. They are variations of throwing techniques, where your own breathing searches and follows that of your partner, and this is what creates the throw.

Those techniques can look very powerful, but they are based on uniting the attacker's and the defender's kokyu, as if breathing jointly. Since breath is the most important driving force in each movement, the joint breathing becomes irresistible.

Breath practice
The way to good belly breathing is not complicated, but demands a lot of effort from most people. You have to remind yourself again and again to lower your breath from

Kokyunage training in Malmö. Tori Jonas Dahlqvist, and uke Tomas Ohlsson. Photo by the author.

the lungs to the abdomen. In the beginning this can even be physically difficult to accomplish. It is tricky to direct one's muscles and organs in something that is normally done without thinking. It will gradually improve through concentration and exercise. One day you will be surprised to discover that you breathe with your lower abdomen, without having to think about it.

It has to start with a good posture. Without the straight back and the protruding belly that the meditating Buddha is always depicted with, you lock your breathing and it never reaches below your chest. The same locking can come from clothes that sit too tightly over your belly. There are many budo practitioners who make the mistake of tying their belt on the waist. Then they cannot learn proper kokyu. You must allow your belly freedom. A strapped belly is just as inhibiting on your breathing as a tightly applied tie around your neck.

When you sit on your knees like in meditation, *zazen*, you are in a good position for finding the correct posture as well as kokyu breathing. The back becomes straight almost automatically, the belly protrudes, and it is not difficult at all to inhale all the way down to your center. The trick is to keep your deep breathing and straight posture when you stand up and start your aikido practice.

For the beginners, it is particularly difficult to remain belly breathing when they get out of breath in intense training. Then they usually start to pant uncontrollably, with short and superficial breaths that only involve the chest – although such breathing is not efficient at all. They simply do not get enough fresh air, no matter how fast their breathing is. The same problem often comes when they really need to exert themselves, by lifting something heavy or pushing something steady, and so on. They may even hold their breath, unawares.

The aikido movements are designed in concord with kokyu, so regular training automatically stimulates the belly breathing. By time you learn to breathe correctly, and you will not understand why you initially found it so difficult.

Kokyu plays such an important part in aikido that you should always strive to turn your belly toward what you focus on – the direction in which you move, or the goal you have with your movement. This is done by attacker and defender alike. Returning to the basic sword cut: In the chudankamae initial position, you hold your sword in front of your belly. Since you grab it with both hands it is not comfortable to move it that far in any other direction than the one your belly is pointing.

In all budo, you always want your belly to point in the direction you act. Only by that can you have maximum control and power in your movements. It seems obvious, since that is how the human anatomy works. Still, many beginners have trouble doing it correctly. Suddenly in the middle of a technique, the belly goes one way and the arms another, and balance is lost. If you feel that the belly is not just following the movements, but is the body part really doing them, like the hub turns the wheel around – then you have good kokyu.

When you exercise your kokyu, the ambition should be to fill your whole body with the flow of breath, and extend it way outside the borders of your body. If you are breathing forcefully with your tanden, others around you should sense it without any sound of your breathing needed. You become a pair of bellows, spreading energy, and still discreet like fresh air sweeping in through an opened window. If you really get going, it should feel like a draft.

Maai – the safe distance   間合

Among the many differences between nationalities, one of the most obvious is the distance people of separate cultures prefer to have to each other in conversations and other everyday communication. In some countries that distance is so short that people can almost sit on each other's lap and still have a relaxed conversation. In other countries, such as the Scandinavian ones, a distance of at least arm's length is needed for the two not to feel crowded.

Comical scenes can take place when people of different cultures interact. One advances, not to be impolitely distanced, and the other retreats, not to feel crowded.

Each of us has a private sphere around our body. We want to be alone and at peace within that sphere, except for moments of voluntary intimacy. Japanese people are used to crowds, so they have learned to live like sardines in a can, and still keep their integrity intact. They have a technique of pretending that others just do not exist. When they do have plenty of space at their disposal, they tend to prefer the same distance Scandinavians need.

Reach

In the Japanese martial arts there is a similar personal sphere, which also has a strategic significance. Two combatants in their initial stances choose a certain distance to each other. It is called *maai*, which can be translated harmony of distance, or distance equilibrium.

*Swedish aikido instructors Jan Nevelius, 6 dan Aikikai, and Jorma Lyly,
5 dan, show an aikiken exercise. Photo by Jöran Fagerlund.*

The concept consists of two kanji pictograms. The first
one implies distance and shows the sun, the beams of which
just barely pass the chink between a pair of swinging doors.
The second part is the same *ai* as in aikido, meaning harmony or joining. Outside of budo use, it is simply translated
as interval.

The sign is also used as a measure of length, which is
about six feet, but the correct distance between two combatants varies according to how tall they are, the martial art
they practice, and what weapons they might hold. The basic
principle of maai is simple: They should be so far from each
other that none of them can reach the other in an attack,
without taking a step forward.

For two unarmed persons this means that if they extend
their arms forward, they reach no more than each other's
hands. Maybe the western custom of shaking hands contains
a ritual with the same significance – the two persons measure out a safe distance to each other.

In the sword arts, where the two duelers stand in the
guard *chudankamae*, with their swords held in front of their
bellies, the sides of their sword tips should meet.

If the two combatants stand closer to each other than maai, none of them has the time to avoid a sudden attack. This also increases the risk of a fight starting purely by accident – a defensive reflex gets the whole thing going, without anybody really intending an attack.

This was the biggest drawback of the so-called terror balance between USA and the Soviet Union, until the latter collapsed in 1989. Advancing technology diminished the time between firing missiles and their reaching the target to mere minutes, so both sides had to constantly keep their hands right above that dreaded button. That gives little time for contemplating one's options.

Sphere

In aikido, this maai is like an invisible sphere around the practitioner. Only when the partner penetrates this sphere does the aikido technique commence. Morihei Ueshiba regarded his sphere as a universe of his, where his laws of nature ruled – therefore, an invasion of it was doomed to fail. An attack that reached inside his universe was unavoidably chained to the orbits of it.

Of course, what rests in the middle of this sphere, this universe, is *tanden*, the body center. Aikido is to practice the sovereignty of the sphere and the center. So, defending against an attack is not a struggle to regain command of one's own universe, but to express this command in a natural way.

The attack must fail, since it is done by intrusion into another person's world. The attacker pierces the periphery of the defender's sphere, and therefore loses control of his own sphere as well as his own center. The circular movements of aikido throw him out of the defender's sphere by methods similar to the centrifugal force. As long as the attacker does not succeed in replacing the defender's center with his own, ha cannot be the strongest or the steadiest.

It can be compared to trying to win a debate in a foreign language. By the intrusion, the attacker is forced to adapt the defender's language. So, how could he manage to take over?

In aikido it is necessary to understand that the rules in operation are those of the defender. Accordingly, the biggest mistake the defender can make is to allow the attacker's rules to take over. This happens if your response is one imitating the action of the attacker, thereby actually submitting to it. Then you have accidentally left your own sphere to become the periphery of the attacker's sphere.

Stay in your center and remain in the middle of your sphere.

Irimi, tenkan – inward, outward 入身 転換

There are really just two ways to move in aikido: inward and outward, like in breathing. And just like in breathing they shall by time emerge into one and the same. But at first you need to know the difference between them.

The inward step is called *irimi* and is by its nature closer to the mentality of the attacker. You step almost straight at your partner, right into his or her sphere. If you are to attack, there is no other way. But it is used also in defense, as a way to forestall, to counter the attack before it is completed.

Being bold enough to take this advancing step against a forceful attacker is at the core of budo. The difficulty of daring this step equals what you can win on it. You forestall the attacker by avoiding and countering the attack in one and the same instant. Irimi is the key to the budo insight that attacking is the worst defense. The attacker has a huge disadvantage, compared to the defender.

The kanji pictogram for irimi consists of the symbol for entering or penetrating, and the sign for the body. So the word means to enter the body, i.e. approach the partner.

The outward step is called *tenkan* and is more in tune with the situation and mild strategy of the defender. The term means to convert or divert. It consists of the kanji for turning around and that for changing. Here you step away from the attack, around and behind the attacker. This way you avoid the attack, simultaneously initiating your counter move by this evasive maneuver. The attacker is suddenly on the periphery of the defender's sphere.

Let us pretend that the two combatants are tied to each other with a rope – the attacker at one end of it, and the defender at the other. A suitable length of the rope, the distance between them, is the correct *maai* – five feet or so. The attacking step leads straight toward the defender, who moves forward and to the side, almost to the position the attacker started from. The rope is stretched anew, and the combatants have changed places, but the dynamics of the movement are such that instead of two spheres with separate centers, the attacker is now in the periphery of the defender. Therefore, he can be led around as naturally as the planets orbit the sun.

This depends mainly on the defender not allowing the movement to halt after the attack, but continuing it in an extended curve. It is similar to how a restive horse is led around the ring – the bridle keeps it in the periphery of the person training it.

It may seem odd to those who have not tried it. These dynamics must be experienced in practice. The attacker loses control because he is the attacker, and because the defender responds with the evasive outward step.

Combined

It is easy to conclude that tenkan is the step that agrees the most with the aikido principles, but also irimi is used – although never exactly in the direction of the opponent. That would only result in a collision.

The aikido irimi enters to the side, which escapes the attack just like the tenkan step does. In both cases the attack will miss its target. By irimi the defender will be to the side of the attacker, facing him. By tenkan the defender will end up by the side of the attacker, almost behind him, and face the same way as the attacker does.

Irimi-tenkan training at Brandbergen, Sweden, in the 1980's. Photo by Magnus Burman.

Actually, almost every aikido technique is a combination of the irimi and the tenkan steps. It starts with an irimi advance, to be followed by the tenkan turn. At the first step you avoid the attack, and at the second you initiate the counter move, the actual aikido technique. By time and diligent practice, the two steps will blend into one inseparable whole, like a single step.

The irimi-tenkan steps are the very hocus pocus formula of the aikido transformation of conflict. You meet the attacker openly by irimi, and you turn and join with him or her by tenkan. You go from conflict to agreement, from aggression to harmony, in two simple steps. So, when you practice these steps, consider the significance of the principles behind them.

Omote, ura – front, back

Most aikido techniques exist in two versions, stressing either the inward *irimi* or the outward *tenkan* step. The version based on irimi is mainly done in front of the attacker, whereas the other version includes moving around to his rear. Most beginners have a hard time telling the two versions apart. It usually takes a year or so of practice to recognize their differences.

When I was at that phase of my development, I tended to unknowingly do the latter version even though our instructor had shown the former. He was quite amused by this. Myself, I would like to believe that it depended on my instinctive search for the softest meeting with the attack. I had learned that this was the ideal of aikido, so I went for the most evasive movement.

In those days, the aikido terminology used in our dojo was not altogether Japanese. The two versions of the aikido techniques were called positive and negative. Those words might still be used in some dojo. The Japanese terms are *omote* and *ura*. In aikido they are sometimes used as synonymous to irimi and tenkan, because of the close connections between them: omote to irimi, and ura to tenkan. But omote and ura are complex concepts with significant meanings far beyond that of aikido terminology.

Omote means approximately front or outside. It originates in the term for the hairy side of a fur, or the surface of a piece of clothing. So, it relates to the outside, the visible and obvious.

Ura stands for opposite side, the rear, the inside, and the hidden. Its origin is the term for the inside of a fur, or the lining of a garment.

The word pair, then, can be compared to the opposites obvious and hidden, or to approach the aikido application: straightforward and evasive, or direct and indirect.

I have never experienced that Japanese instructors have considered some moral aspects to this, although to a western mind that seems near at hand. Instead, my impression is that they regard it as the two sides of a coin. In aikido, omote and ura are as complimentary and mutually dependent as the inside and outside of a garment.

During practice, it is beneficiary to acquaint oneself with the specific characteristics of these opposites. The omote form of an aikido technique can be done in an almost pushy way, with a spirit of eagerly meeting the attack – still with the evasive body movement, *taisabaki*, so that you do not confront the oncoming force. Then the ura version should be done so that you already at the initial meeting more or less disappear from the attacker's eyesight, into the shadows.

These opposites can be compared to the Chinese *yin* and *yang*, in Japanese *in* and *yo*. Their initial meaning of shady side and sunny side show obvious parallels to ura and omote. When you do the omote version, your attitude should be comparable to yang, which is described as the extrovert, the light, the warm, and traditionally linked to the masculine. Accordingly, the ura version should resemble yin, which stands for the introvert, the dark, the cold, and traditionally the female. Of course, the traditional gender roles in this can be discussed.

Shoden, okuden

Another pair of opposites, vaguely linked to omote and ura, are the budo concepts *shoden* and *okuden*. Shoden is the front or first teaching, and okuden is the inner or deep teaching. Some traditional budo arts stressed this division greatly, so that the beginner was for a long time only taught shoden techniques, before he or she was regarded as mature enough to exercise okuden techniques. There is still such a division in some iaido and kenjutsu schools, but usually there is no restriction against beginners trying okuden early on.

In aikido there is no division of the techniques into shoden and okuden. I have the impression that such thinking would be very alien to Osensei's mind. He was rather restrictive about teaching counter moves to the aikido techniques, *kaeshiwaza*, to others than instructors, but apart from that he seemed to make no specific distinction between aikido for beginners and for the advanced. Maybe to him all students were beginners.

Miyamoto Musashi, the legendary samurai of the 17th century, had no respect for shoden and okuden thinking in the martial arts. He stated in his still widely read *Book of Five Rings*: "In real battle there is no such thing as fighting with an outer technique and cutting with an inner technique." He admitted that there are simpler and deeper things in the martial arts, and it varies how the students manage to grasp them, but he refused the idea that the techniques could be sorted accordingly. The inner and the outer are unavoidably mixed: "If you go deeper and deeper into the mountain, eventually you will again find yourself at the entrance."

It would definitely be a mistake to regard the omote version of an aikido technique as shoden, and the ura form as okuden. Any technique, in whatever version, has obvious aspects and hidden ones. It contains easily attainable elements as well as obscure ones. The more you practice aikido, the more complex it all gets.

I am also not that keen on regarding omote and ura as versions applicable to different situations. For example, it is often said that the ura form of a technique comes in handy when the partner somehow succeeds to resist the omote form. True, but a better way of dealing with the situation is to find a way of making the omote form work, in spite of the resistance. We have a greater chance of improving our ways of doing the techniques, if we work with the assumption that they can be done in any situation.

Maybe the omote and ura pair should be regarded as a way of getting to know the essence of a certain technique better, by sort of seeing it from two angles.

Gotai – static training   固体

Generally speaking, there are three ways of training aikido: *gotai*, *jutai*, and *kinagare* – static, soft, and flowing. Although they can be described as three stages in the development of the aikido student, they are constantly present and intermingled in aikido practice. They complement each other.

Gotai (also pronounced *kotai*) translates to hard body,

French teacher Christian Tissier, 7 dan Aikikai shihan, demonstrating
morotedori at a Stockholm seminar. Photo by Magnus Hartman.

referring to a static kind of training. Each technique commences from both practitioners standing still. Uke is allowed
to grab hold of tori before the latter starts with the aikido
technique. Of course, this is not the best kind of self-defense,
but utterly important for tori to learn to manage. And for the
beginner, gotai is the only chance to try out the complicated
aikido techniques, and get acquainted with them.

For lots of years, Japanese budo practitioners have
enjoyed trying to get out of all kinds of grips and holds.
Aikido is highly respected because of the ease by which it
gets you out of even very hard grips.

To the samurai it was particularly essential to break free
of holds that hindered them from drawing their swords, just
as it was desirable for their opponents to lock their hands.
That is why aikido, which has grown out of the samurai arts,
contains many techniques against wrist grips. Practicing
against such attacks is also particularly good for experienc-
ing the aikido principles and methods. In these cases, the
inner workings of the techniques become quite evident.

If you do not know how, it can be very tricky to get out

Aikido

of strong wrist grips – and in gotai the partner should hold quite firmly. Of course, you can have the same problem with all kinds of holds – embraces, chokes, and so on. Those who are the biggest and the strongest seem to have all the winning cards. Aikido can change that.

Use your center
In gotai there are two aikido principles mainly at work against the strong holds: The first is to always keep your center behind what you do, and the other is to discover the potential movement hidden also inside the most rigid situation.

Turn your belly and center, *tanden*, toward the target, so that it becomes a support and a launching pad for any movement. That is of at least as much help as learning to lift heavy things with your legs instead of your back. All movements in aikido should come from tanden in the lower abdomen. To learn this, make sure that you always turn your belly in the direction you want to move. This is done by body turns, especially with flexibility in the hips.

It is not that difficult to hold somebody's arms or legs or head, but it is next to impossible to prevent somebody from moving his or her hips. You can almost always move your hips – even if several strong persons hold you – and thereby you get the flexibility needed to get out of any grip. Through turning your hips you find the way out, and by keeping your belly pointing in that direction, you get enough power and stability to move that way.

Though the hips seem to be doing the job, it is important to continue focusing on the belly – to find one's center and to keep from losing balance and stability. Without a good balance you are unlikely to get out of any grip. Actually, the strongest of two combatants will usually be the one with the best balance – independently of muscle size. Like the boa constrictor needs to fasten the tip of its tail in order to squeeze its prey, man must have balance to use his strength. And the balance is always based in the body center, tanden, which is also the center of mass.

Therefore it is only through your partner's center that you can influence his balance, and this is necessary to lead him into the orbits of the aikido techniques, getting you free. There is always movement inside your partner's belly, potential movement in any conceivable direction. This can be awakened and guided, no matter how rigidly your partner seems to stand or how firm his grip is.

Movement is awakened by relaxation. Oddly, that is the opposite of what people usually do when someone grabs them. They tighten their muscles, tear and pull, trying to break free. That only makes your partner stronger, and the grip tightens. But when you relax and become soft, then the partner's grip loses its stability, and you can trace the many potential directions in which to move him or her. You only need to choose.

This natural law is easy to try out. If you let your partner grab your wrist really hard, while you tighten your fist and the muscles on your arm – then both can feel how strong your partner's grip is. But if you suddenly open your hand and relax all your muscles, then your partner's grip sort of slips, and loses its strength. He or she must renew the grip, put new force to it, to regain control. It is easy for you to start your aikido technique before that happens.

Soft and supple are almost synonymous. When you are soft you can move in just about any direction, whatever the obstacle. Softness is real strength.

Jutai – soft training   柔体

The word *go* in gotai really means hard, but for the aikido application of the term, the word static is more accurate. But the next step, *jutai*, is a clear opposite of the hard. *Ju* means soft. It is the same word as in judo and jujutsu.

Jutai is the soft style of training, and it comes as a logical consequence of the static training. Gotai opens for the

Iriminage at Järfälla dojo in the 1970's. Photo by the author.

soft way. Actually, it develops into softness all by itself, as you progress in your aikido. The hard grip softens and dissolves. The rigid position is transformed into supple waves of motion. Your heightened skills make gotai look more and more like jutai.

Still, in jutai the soft training is the starting point. You initiate your aikido technique before the attack has reached you, before the attacker's grip is completed. When your partner advances toward you in the attack, you simultaneously take the first step of your aikido technique. Only at the moment before the attack commences are both of you still.

Taisabaki

Your first step is the advancing and at the same time evading *taisabaki* movement of irimi or tenkan, omote or ura. In this step, as in any other aikido movement, the direction of your belly and the movements of your hips are most important. When your hips turn, you disappear as a target, sort of like a door opening. You end up at the side of the partner with you belly pointing at him or her.

Thereby you have a priceless advantage. Your partner is aimed straight ahead, in the direction where you, the target, were in the previous moment. But you are well inside the attacker's sphere, with all your power aimed at him. It takes a comparatively long time for the attacker to redirect his power and body toward your present position, and during that time you are quite free to do just about anything that comes to mind.

What comes to mind is an aikido technique, which continues to lead your partner's power in a direction where it causes no harm. Only if your partner manages to halt his flow of power and arrest his movement, will he be able to redirect his attack. The aikido technique gives him no such opportunity. What it does is to lead him on in the original attack, farther than he had planned, but with a kind of hopefulness remaining, so that in his body he feels that he is still about to defeat his opponent – although he no longer has any clue as to how.

In jutai there are only two static moments. One is before the attack commences, when the two practitioners watch each other at the correct distance, *maai*. The other moment is at the end of the technique, when the attacker is held in a pinning or thrown to the floor.

What is most of all trained in jutai is taisabaki, the body turn that makes the attacker miss his target, and simultaneously begins the aikido technique. Compared to gotai you have simply started your hip movement, and thereby your step, at an earlier moment. This move, which did in gotai lead to your release from the hard grip, is in jutai what makes the attacker fail to apply the grip completely.

Jutai is the normal way of doing the aikido techniques. Also, its timing makes it possible to defend against strikes, hits, and kicks. For obvious reasons, that is not suitable to do from a static position. In addition, practicing jutai automatically leads away from doing the techniques step by step. Your aikido changes into one where all the steps of your technique blend, to become one joint movement. Then it approaches *kinagare*.

Kinagare – flowing training　氣流

The attentive reader has already concluded that the difference between static, soft, and flowing aikido training, has less to do with how the techniques are done than with when they are initiated. Gotai starts when the attacker's grip is properly applied, and jutai when the attack is commenced but not completed. *Kinagare* has no starting point.

The aim of aikido is never to get stuck in a self-defense situation, a battle between two wills. No matter how big an advantage you may have, there is a risk in accepting the challenge, and at the end of the fight there is a bitter loser, whether it is you or the other person. No, in aikido we want to reach a state that cannot be disturbed by aggression, not shaken by challenge, and in no need to take cover afore hostility. You just walk on, as if nothing happened.

That is *kinagare* (or *ki no nagare*, as it is sometimes written), a constant flow of ki. The attacker is sucked into this flow, and led away, without the defender having to halt or change course. The aikido techniques are done during the walk, without any distinguishable beginning or end. Only the attacker is able to point out some kind of start – that of his own attack.

Taninzugake
When there are several attackers, which is called *taninzugake*, it is both natural and necessary to shift to kinagare, which does not stop at someone or contain a foreseeable strategy. It is quite entertaining to watch, when well done: The aikidoist wanders about randomly in a crowd of adversaries, who all miss their target, tumbling this way and that, like bowling pins at a strike. But the aikido principles are clear and not that difficult to apply in such a situation. Actually, it is more difficult to be one of the attackers, who runs a risk of being hit by one of his companions, and has a hard time indeed to keep track of the defender.

In kinagare, this natural flow of ki and the body move-

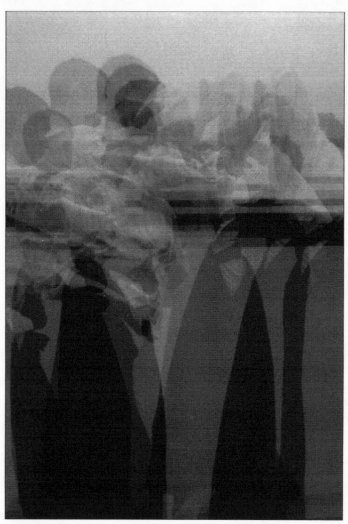

Aikido training in the author's dojo Enighet, Sweden. Photo by Gisela Döhler.

ments are trained by continuous taisabaki. Because you never stay on one and the same spot, the attackers are unable to join in an ordered charge, and because you always make irimi and tenkan moves, no individual attacker will succeed with his strike.

You can also observe the clever way the aikido techniques are constructed. They are such that all through doing them, you move in repeated taisabaki, so that surrounding attackers miss if they try to strike you when you do your technique on one of them. This was a necessary component for the martial arts of the samurai, since they prepared not only for duels, but for the battlefield as well.

The most common techniques in kinagare are the throws, because they are quick and do not demand that you stop in some position. But the pinning techniques can also work against several attackers, although slightly modified. For example, they can easily be converted to throws or quick felling techniques, or they can be used to put one attacker in the way of the others. And the pinning techniques, too, can be done in a series of taisabaki evasions.

Still, all the aikido techniques get a more flowing character in kinagare – spirals and ellipses that are like whirlwinds as they fell the attackers, also often those who are not actually touched by the aikido techniques.

Of course it is also possible to practice kinagare one on one. Then the attacker has to hurry to get up after each felling, to attack anew. The defender should always be on the move, and preferably toward the partner instead of away from him or her, so that the tempo increases. It can be quite a demanding kind of training.

Another rewarding way of raising the tempo is by *kakarigeiko*, where several attackers stand in line, and hurry forward one after the other, as soon as the defender has thrown the previous attacker – or better: right before the defender has done so. With this kind of training, you also learn to adapt immediately to different attackers' temper, size, strength, and so on.

Improvisation

In high tempo kinagare it is impossible to do your techniques with your conscious mind. The brain is far too slow a commander. The initiative has to come from the reflexes and the intuition. You release your flow and let the aikido techniques express this naturally, following the flow where it happens to go. It can be compared to improvisation in music, where the brain is far behind the rapid advancement of the fingers on the instrument.

Certainly, kinagare is the training form that comes the closest to the essence of aikido. The aikidoist should always be in the middle of this flow, which automatically leads to techniques as soon as somebody attacks – and it happens immediately, naturally, as if the whole chain of events had been prepared and learned by heart. Contrary to this impression, it is impossible to accomplish such aikido by preparation and rehearsal. It must be born unprepared, out of a center awake and living.

When this works, less and less of physical contact is needed to do the aikido technique. You become like a current that the attacker is sucked into. Neither pinning techniques nor throws demand physical exertion, or a firm grip on the attacker. It just flows.

Although to those who do not yet comprehend it, this seems like unreliable self-defense, it is the way to an aikido that is really fascinating – both to the one doing it, and the one it is done to. Eventually, you should be able to treat your partner with the same ease as the conductor leads an orchestra – maybe one day also at the same distance.

Zanshin – extended spirit

When in *kinagare* you go like a whirlwind among the attackers, it easily happens that tenderness and care get lost. The attackers are thrown around and into one another, leading

Former doshu Kisshomaru Ueshiba (1921-1999), the son of Osensei, at an aikido demonstration in Aiki Jinja, the small temple beside the dojo in Iwama.

to injuries and bitterness. That is no good. The benevolent aikidoist wants to protect the attackers from unnecessary harm. There should be no retribution. It is enough to show the attackers a better course of action than the malice they intended. Nobody should get hurt. Instead, everybody should learn, and leave the fight as wiser and more placid persons.

Therefore, an aikido technique does not end with the throw, but is extended all through the trajectory of the falling attacker, remaining with him until he chooses to interrupt his malice and walk away. The aikidoist's attention and ki flow continue to encircle and lead the attacker all through the throw, making sure that it is lenient. Also, the continued attention makes sure that the attacker becomes aware of what the laws are in the defender's sphere, the aikidoist's universe.

Judo has the same friendly spirit, which is shown in how the thrower holds up the thrown partner's arm, so that he will land safely on the side, and not hit his head. In aikido we rarely hold on to the person we throw, but with the direction of the movement and with our ki, we show the best way for the fall. It is not enough to throw the attacker. We also make sure to cushion the fall. Correctly done, the aikido throws are not that unpleasant to the victims of them. They fall just as softly as they are snared in the pinning techniques.

Remaining

This is accomplished by *zanshin*, extended spirit. This concept is particularly stressed in karatedo, but is also significant in aikido. It consists of two kanji pictograms: *zan* means to remain, and *shin* (also pronounced *kokoro*) means heart, mind, or spirit. A remaining spirit. Concentration that does not falter.

In Japan, the heart is used in connection to countless things. Contrary to western use of the word, it rarely has anything to do with emotions, but with willpower, mentality, and spirit. Zanshin means not to lose contact with the partner in the throw. Your attention remains when you lost physical contact with your partner, sort of how in javelin you follow the flight of the spear until it pierces the ground. It definitely has a martial aspect. The defender guards and controls the attacker all the way until the latter is no longer a threat. With forceful zanshin it is even possible to deter the other from attacking anew.

It is also with zanshin that the partner is controlled in a pinning. Zanshin is the force of attention and resolve, showing one's center and remaining in it. You continue to surround and penetrate your partner with your ki, so that no other courses are accessible than the ones you have marked out. That makes the partner immovable in a pinning, and kind of stunned after a throw, having a hard time standing up again – as if you were standing over him, pressing him to the ground.

Protection

The friendlier side of zanshin is also practical. By extending your attention beyond the reach of the aikido technique, it becomes harder for the partner to resist, and the technique is free of weaknesses. By guiding the partner's fall with your mind, he is unable to change its course. By applying the extended spirit of zanshin to the pinning, it becomes solid without needing to inflict pain on the partner.

Zanshin is the clear and decisive spirit that shall reach and penetrate the partner already before the attack, so that it comes as the defender wishes. Of course, it must remaing during the attack, and after it. Zanshin is the defender's connection to the attacker, and it should be like that of a ruler to his or her subject – a kind ruler, with compassion for the subject. Noble zanshin is not exclusively for the protection of the defender. Also the attacker is protected and preserved by it. When your zanshin becomes like pure benevolence, I doubt that it is possible to attack you at all.

Uke – the one who is led

Although only the defense techniques are aikido, still the attacker's role is not to be neglected. The kind of attack and the skill of it are also of importance. Because aikido itself contains no attack techniques, it is common that the students train them insufficiently, and do them with little concentration. But sloppy and weak attacks lead to sloppy and weak aikido. Both roles are important, because aikido is about guiding the attacking force.

The attacker in aikido is called *uke*, like in the term for falling technique: *ukemi*. The kanji for uke is a sign that means to receive and be susceptible. The symbols that compose the sign show a hand giving something. So, the attacker is the one who is led, who is receiving.

The defender, the one who leads, is called *tori* – or *nage*, as in *nagewaza*, throwing techniques. Tori simply means to take. Amusingly, it is written with the symbols of somebody grabbing the ear of another – an action that seems to be comparable to the western use of it, and therefore implies a correcting purpose, like that of a teacher or parent.

Observe that the word pair tori and uke does not signify give and take, but take and receive. So, the two have similar roles in the aikido training. The difference is that tori has the initiative, although uke is the one who starts it off with the attack. In aikido, then, you should take over the initiative – not to win, but for both to learn something. Since this means so much more than just throwing somebody, I prefer the word tori, not nage. Still, both words are used for the defender in aikido.

Tori's role is that of the placid one, who calmly awaits the attack and then neutralizes it as pleasantly as possible. Naturally, the attacker's role is quite different. He or she is supposed to charge with complete concentration and maximum skill. Inferior attacks result in bad training and disharmony in the aikido techniques.

The author showing maegeri, front kick, on David Bradna, at a seminar in Pardubice, Czech Republic. Photo by Leos Matousek.

Attacking spirit

It is not easy to be a good uke. You need to master a number of attack techniques, *kogeki*, usually brought in from the other budo arts – such as punches and kicks from karatedo, sword strikes from kendo, grips from judo, and so on. It is not enough to lazily hint these techniques, just because you know that you are going to miss and get thrown. Each time, you must attack wholeheartedly and forcefully, without any thought on what the defense will be.

This usually works fine the first time you practice a certain aikido technique, but already when uke stands up again for a second attack, his attitude and approach have changed. Uke knows what technique will be done on him, so he unconsciously redirects his attack slightly – either to make it more difficult for the partner to do the aikido technique, or to make it easier and more comfortable. Unfortunately, from that moment on the training is a bit falsified.

Aikido is not as much about the physiology of extended arms and charging bodies, as it is about energies and laws inside of the bodily manifestations. Therefore it is important that the spirit of the attack is correct. Uke must adapt the spirit of an attacker, and express it consistently. The strikes are aimed right at the defender, and the grips strive to hold the defender – just like in a fight. Of course, the attacker still needs to show the same care as the defender does, so that no one gets harmed.

Uke should exert himself to act like a great samurai: advance with the center, let his ki flow, and show firm determination. Aikido is constructed to work against the best and most skilled attack, and the most competent challenger. Only when uke tries his utmost to be all that, tori is given a chance to develop an aikido with such superiority.

Uke must all through the technique remain in an attacking spirit. Many practitioners make a forceful initial charge, but relax as soon as tori starts with the responding aikido technique. They become almost lifeless weights to throw or lead down to a pinning. That is not natural. The will to attack shall remain all through, so that if tori makes some mistake in the aikido technique, it is possible for uke to get free and attack anew.

This may seem like an aggressive game, but it is exactly what the aikido techniques are made to handle. That is the path to the softest and most pleasant techniques. Aikido should transform aggression into peacefulness. If the former is never present, there is no way of learning how to make the transformation.

A competent attack follows the same principles as the aikido defense techniques. The body center, *tanden*, is the base, and *ki* is the energy that constitutes the true attack. Uke shall strive for good balance and control, turn his belly in the direction he is moving, and never lose concentration. He shall try to keep the initiative – attack where he can, and protect himself where he feels threatened.

When learning how to attack correctly, you will benefit from studying and appreciating how this is done in the budo arts that train attacks as much as defense. So, for punches and kicks, look at karatedo, for grips study judo, for sword techniques consider kendo and iaido, for staff techniques see jodo, and so on. The more familiar you are with other mar-

Present doshu Moriteru Ueshiba, Osensei's grandson, at a Stockholm demonstration. Photo by Magnus Hartman.

tial arts – and not only the Japanese ones – the trustworthier your aikido solutions will become.

Grabbing a wrist

The seemingly most simple of attacks is *katatedori*, grabbing the defender's wrist. It is actually just as demanding and complex as any other attack. Uke takes a quick step forward and catches tori's wrist in a steady grip, which stops the hand from retreating as well as from attacking uke. So, the grip is both a defense and an attack. Also, it is easily followed up by a strike with the free hand.

To grab somebody is to tie him or her to one's center, similar to holding a dog by a leash. You take a steady stance and strive to control your partner's body and movements through the grip. As with the sword guard *chudankamae*, you apply your grip in front of your center, and should be able to maneuver your partner's arm as freely as you would a sword in your hand.

Grabbing your partner's wrist is in many ways similar to holding your sword. In your grip, the little finger is the most important one and should be tied the hardest around the partner's wrist. Your balance and the power of your grip are rooted in your center, and you should be able to immediately change your own position as well as that of the arm you hold.

If the defender tries to break free with a strike, his arm can easily be used to parry the strike. If the defender tries to tear himself away, the grip will tighten and he will lose his balance. By the grip, the attacker aims to bring the defender into his sphere, his universe. This cannot be accomplished with tense muscles, but by relaxation and a focused spirit. Then it will be quite difficult for tori to get free. The harmonious way of aikido must be applied.

All through the aikido technique, the attacker strives to keep this control. As much as he can, he tries to turn his belly toward the wrist grip, and continues to direct his ki, his attacking power, toward the defender. When the aikido technique is done in a slow tempo, this can seem strained and exaggerated, but when it is done in normal speed it becomes obvious that this attitude is the only possible one. Aikido works in such a way that the attacker is unable to interrupt the attack before the technique is completed.

The attacker's defense

With increasing refinement as you develop, your aikido defense uses one circumstance that is evident to any attacker: The one who attacks must count on being vulnerable, too. The one who strives to hurt someone else also runs the risk of being hurt. So, the attacker wants to protect himself as well as win the fight. Any attack includes some kind of defense.

Many aikido techniques are built on the body's and the mind's basic struggle to survive. The instinct to protect oneself overshadows any conscious ambition and any trained series of movements. Also the most lionhearted champion has reflexes that twitch in him when sensitive parts of the body are exposed to threats. Thereby the defender can manipulate the attacker.

But these reflexes can only be used when uke is as concentrated on attacking, as he would be if it were done in actual malice. So, uke must imitate this feeling when attacking. There is no need to pounce like a rabid dog at the defender, because that only leads to injuries and a very unpleasant atmosphere in the dojo. It has to remain a controlled pretense. Uke can accomplish this by being focused on the attack, and remaining ignorant of what the defender aims to do – no matter how many times it is repeated. Uke shall react to the aikido techniques as if unprepared for them.

Practice in such a spirit is an effective way of emptying one's mind of thoughts. That is a budo way to emptiness and clarity. Also, taking turns with attacking and defending is excellent training in directing one's ki and controlling one's temper. At one moment you are uke, a forceful and intense attacker, and the next moment you are tori, the placid and gentle defender. That opens for a calm soul.

Keiko – practice, practice, practice 稽古

I have surely at least implied, here and there in this book, that a book about aikido never can do justice to the training of it. Nor can it adequately present any of the aspects of aikido and its content. This book might be of some use as an introduction for those who speculate about what aikido can be, but even as such it is a bit misleading, since it cannot convey the experience of aikido training.

The book may serve as extracurricular material for the aikido practitioner with a hunger for knowledge – but then there is a risk that the aikido student exaggerates the importance of thinking, of theoretical pursuit, as if it were at least as essential as practical training. Nothing could be more wrong.

Japanese teachers are usually restrictive when it comes to talking about aikido philosophy and principles. On direct

Tatami, the mat, is prepared for a seminar in Plzen, Czech Republic. Photo by Antonín Knízek.

questions about what this or that might signify, or why we do in one way and not the other, their answer is often simply: "You just have to practice." They have a thought behind this, if not to say a complete philosophy.

Man is a whole being. The intellect and the body are not isolated from each other, nor is one disconnected while the other one is at work. While we practice, we think constantly – analyze, interpret, conclude, and gradually understand. But when we read or sit down to discuss aikido, then the body has nothing to do. It is locked out, unable to contribute with anything else than the itch for training that every aikido student is familiar with, and experiences already the day after an aikido class – at the very latest. Therefore it is always more rewarding to practice, even when the most abstract and theoretical questions about aikido occupy the mind.

Keiko is the Japanese word for training, used in all the budo arts. It is written with two kanji that collectively translate simply as training or study. But like so often with kanji, more is told when they are examined closer. The first one means to consider, and the second one means old, what has existed for long. We should consider the old, i.e. contemplate the tradition. So, although the word is used for physical training, which may very well be quite exerting to the body, its etymology refers clearly to a thought process. What is emphasized is that by physical practice you can gain clarity of the mind.

Certainly, also theoretical studies have their place. They satisfy our curiosity, and curiosity is the best guide we have in life. We just need to remember that it is first and foremost by training in the dojo that we gain the true insights. That is where our knowledge can be properly expressed. Only by practice do the theories become understandable.

Takemusu – limitless improvisation 武産

Aikido of today is well organized, with a hierarchy, rules for kyu and dan grading, and a system of basic techniques that are to be done in a somewhat regulated way. But this neat order is not the work of Morihei Ueshiba. He never wanted to deal with the politics and administration of the martial art he invented. He graded people spontaneously, almost on a whim – also the highest grades. And he did not construct a system of basic techniques. Mostly he just said, now and then during class: "This is a basic technique in aikido." His students hurried to make notes.

To Morihei Ueshiba, budo was something quite separate from the worldly order. The secrets of budo – and for a long time he was rather restrictive about them – were only to be transmitted from the teacher to the students in everyday dojo practice. Anything else lacked significance. There was no particular pedagogic system on the agenda. To Osensei, aikido was nothing but the pleasant expression of pure spirit and divine principles. The techniques had no other value to him than as links to that higher and inner essence. So why make a big deal out of them?

Aikido is not to settle with a number of fixed throws and pinnings. On the contrary, it must become *takemusu*, a limitless martial art born in the moment. Improvisation.

Creative

Takemusu consists of two words. *Take* is identical with *bu* in budo, the martial way. It is just another pronunciation of it. *Musu* (also pronounced *umu*) means approximately to give birth, to procreate, as in pregnancy and childbirth. The expression takemusu can simply be translated as creative martial art. The creativity of it implies variation and the ability to adapt. Then there is no number of basic techniques that suffices. Aikido should be born in the moment, improvised out of the circumstances, so that there is never a repeated predictable pattern.

The basic techniques are primarily exercises in finding one's center and getting one's ki flowing. When you have practiced aikido for some time, you notice increasingly how new ways of doing the techniques emerge, and this stimulates experiments. You feel constant movement inside yourself. It originates in *tanden*, your body center. When this inner movement is expressed, it leads effortlessly to aikido techniques. Sometimes these techniques are the familiar basics, and sometimes they are so different that you will not know what to call them.

Unfortunately, the ordered form of training and grading in aikido tends to obstruct this spontaneity and improvisation. Of course, you need to practice the basic techniques so that you become skilled at them, and continue to train them so that you can do them with increased refinement. But you must also break their patterns. Variation and open-minded discovery!

Variations

One way to stimulate this power of the imagination in aikido is to try several of the existing variations to basic techniques. Experienced aikido teachers can show tens of variations on any of the basic techniques. It is rather strenuous to remem-

Swedish instructor Åke Bengtsson, 5 dan Aikikai, at an outdoor training. Photo by Magnus Hartman.

ber them all, so you try them and then forget them. They will be reborn naturally another time, like improvisations and sudden whims. Also other variations, previously untried, will emerge just as easily during practice.

You should not really memorize and plan your aikido practice way ahead. That only becomes a burden and creates limitations. Instead, dare to trust that your center contains all, and lets it emerge at the right moment. If you empty your head of thoughts, and trust your inner capacity, so much will emerge that you soon become your own richest source and foremost teacher.

Some aikido instructors get so delighted by the variations they invent, or learned from their own teachers, that they start to systematize and memorize them. They teach the variations with the same sternness and care as they do with the original basic techniques. This has little to do with takemusu. What does a musician gain from writing down and rehearsing his improvisations, until he has learned them by heart?

Takemusu is by its nature similar to ki: Let the ideas fly

off as quickly as they came, and there will be more. The flow is what is important.

When Morihei Ueshiba talked about *takemusu aiki*, he must have meant that the harmonious way of aikido naturally gives birth to an endlessly innovative martial art. The joint spirit of *tori* and *uke* in aiki leads to limitless budo. Just by taking the initial step of *irimi* or *tenkan*, past the attacking force of the partner but still in rhythm with it, a solution will immediately appear to the defender. The technique that comes to mind will be both effective and soft. The principles of aiki and the evasive movement become a gate that opens to a world of possibilities.

Nen – one with the moment 念

The concept most difficult to explain, among those used in budo philosophy, is *nen*. That may be the reason for it being rarely used in texts as well as in dojo training. Still, let us try.

The kanji for nen is composed of two words: one is *ima*, which means now, the present, and the other is *kokoro* (also pronounced *shin*), representing the heart, but also the mind or spirit. In western symbolism, the heart is usually described as the seat of emotions. But in Japanese tradition, the will and the mentality are what belong there.

The difference is not altogether insurmountable. Following one's heart, which is a European ideal, and trusting what the heart dictates, comes very near to the Japanese concept. Willpower and intention are expressions of the heart. Pure at heart, you go straight ahead without hesitation, without ever being diverted.

Nen, the combined concept, can in an everyday context be translated as thought, idea, sense, wish, concern, and such. Generally speaking, it means suddenly getting an idea or sentiment. The mind is in the present, the moment of the willpower. The heart is filled with only one purpose.

More clues are given by how nen is combined with other words in more complex concepts. *Sennen* means to be absorbed or completely devoted to something. *Nenjiru* means prayer, *neniri* concern, and *nengan* means an inner wish, one's heart's desire, which is also called *ichinen*. So, in all cases nen is connected to the will and the mental attitude.

The moment

In aikido, the meaning of nen is extended and deepened. It becomes a guiding rule for the mental attitude, how the mind should operate during practice. First and foremost, you have to be wholeheartedly concentrated on nothing but what you are involved in at the moment. All your attention, and all your senses, should be focused on what is at hand, what you are in the middle of.

Although the word nen is difficult to interpret, understanding it is not as tricky as actually practicing it. Just like in meditation, you can quickly notice how irrelevant things pop up in your mind and disturb your practice. The five senses seem to cooperate with the brain in interfering with the training. They have to be cleaned and restrained, similar to how you in *kiai* gather all your ki for one purpose.

But keeping the mind clean and fixed on the aikido training are really just negations, and therefore not complete explanations of what nen is. When the mind is focused like this, nen develops into an insight and certainty, which will breed an aikido with the elegance of the endlessly evident. You do not have to ponder and analyze, nor do you need to prepare or process. It comes automatically.

Children often function like that with their knowledge and thinking. Ask a mathematically gifted child how it solved a certain calculation, and the response will often be "Because it is so," or "I just knew." With a pure mind and a concentration solely on the task of the moment, the answer often comes as quickly and readily as if angels whispered in one's ear.

Perhaps the Greek philosopher Plato pointed out the same mental ability, when he stated that man is born with all knowledge already in his mind – he just has to be reminded of it. Then nen is that reminded state of mind, when you need neither to search through the brain for an answer, nor test your body in order to find the next step. It comes naturally, at once.

Perception

You do not need to practice aikido that very long before you experience moments of significantly sharpened perception, and a considerably increased speed of your reflexes. An attack that turns out differently than you expected, automatically leads to another defense technique than you had prepared to do. Also attacks completely without warning can be escaped in the same manner, although you have no idea how you manage.

Nen gives a capacity that can very well be compared to what we call the sixth sense. You are able of much more than you could imagine, and you perceive things that your eyes and ears are hardly equipped to register. It is not at all reached by the power and sharpness of thought. On the contrary, it demands that you empty your mind of will and assumptions. You have to become as blank as a newborn child.

Morihei Ueshiba told his students that by time, he got a sixth sense that functioned almost like radar. When an attacker set out to charge, Ueshiba perceived sort of a white flash of light, preceding the attack. Thereby, he had plenty of time to avoid it. It did not matter if the attacker was in sight or not. The white flash always warned him.

You can also perceive it as an itch or a vague tickling sensation, when a threat emerges – even if that threat is no more than an idea in the head of the attacker. And if you happen to show a gap in your defense, you can feel it as sort of a tickling in the part of the body that is not protected. To reach this sensitivity, you must lower the noise of your brain, so that you perceive the faint signals. You empty your mind of thoughts. Instead you trust your inner capacity and collect yourself in your center.

Shoji Nishio (1927-2005), 8 dan Aikikai shihan, shows his irimi entrance and atemi strike at a mid-1990's seminar in the author's dojo. Photo by Ulf Lundquist.

Morihei Ueshiba said that nen becomes a link between man and the great whole, so that there is no longer anything out of reach for the perception. That is to become one with the universe, the natural. Therefore, you have to practice without purpose, without selfishness or preconceptions.

Those who cannot throw away their ambitions will constantly be disturbed and inhibited by them. Only the one who is completely unbiased can accept whatever comes his or her way, and adapt to it without difficulty. When you make your mind empty, it has room for everything that comes, and perceives even the weakest signals. So, nen is to make the mind empty, to throw away your thoughts, and let your aikido be born exactly in the moment – as if it did not exist beforehand, as if nothing existed beforehand.

Kototama – the soul of words 言霊

There is an American TV documentary from 1958 named *Rendez-vous with Adventure*, where two sturdy men in cowboy hats visit Hombu dojo, the aikido headquarters in Tokyo. They travel around the world in search for exciting challenges for real men, and get curious about this strange martial art and its old founder.

At this time Morihei Ueshiba was around 75 years of age, which did not stop him from waltzing around for a while with one of the tall Americans. When they sit down for a conversation, the TV reporters ask what is really behind aikido, what principles are at the core of it, and how the old man who is about half their size can perform such feats. Ueshiba points at a drawn circle on the table in front of them, and says that every circle must have a center – otherwise it cannot be drawn. The TV men mumble something confused in response.

Then Ueshiba continues to speak solely about *kototama* (often spelled *kotodama*). Koichi Tohei, who used to assist Ueshiba in those days, has a hard time trying to translate it with his limited knowledge of the English language. Finally, Ueshiba gives an example of the mysticism of sounds that is the essence of kototama, chanting a long vowel sound at the same time as he uses his fan to draw a cross in the air.

Kototama was really the subtle core of Osensei's aikido, and occasionally he held long lectures on the subject to his students. They understood little more than the American TV reporters did. Fortunately, he never demanded of his students to study this doctrine as he had done. On the contrary, he disapproved when students tried to repeat his spiritual exercises. He interrupted them with the words: "Don't copy me!"

Nonetheless, in his soul and heart aikido was undoubtedly an expression of the cosmology he had found in kototama. His aikido was essentially a religious practice, based on the principles of kototama. Ueshiba had an ardently religious view on the world, based on Shinto and influenced by the many years he had spent with the religious movement Omotokyo.

Vibrations
In traditional Shinto, there is a system of cosmology and mysticism called *kototama*, describing the world through sounds and vibrations. Kototama can be translated as the soul or spirit of the words. It is a system of vowels, consonants, and combinations thereof, where every sound has its meaning and underlying significance. When the sounds are combined and pronounced, their underlying powers get into play, through the working of their vibrations. They carry their specific meaning and express it when pronounced.

In kototama these sounds and what they signify are exercised, as a form of meditation or purification ceremony. They are chanted, like prayer or *mantra*, the Indian form of meditation on sounds. But according to kototama, the powers of the sounds are active also when pronounced in regular speech – whether the speaker is aware of this or not.

Old roots
The system is certainly very old, and has grown to almost impenetrable complexity. In addition, there are several different schools of it, although the basic principles are the same. Kototama gets its cosmology out of the Japanese religious sources *Kojiki* and *Nihongi*, from the 8th century. The long names of the gods, and the adventures they have in these books, are in kototama regarded as keys to how the world was created, and what laws rule it – for men as well as gods.

Similar mystic systems are found in other religions, such as Buddhism and Hinduism, or in the Jewish teaching of *kabbalah*. Also the anthroposophy movement, founded by Rudolf Steiner in the early 20th century, attaches certain values to the different sounds and letters.

In Christianity, fragments of related thoughts can be observed, for example in the first lines of the Gospel of John:

Taninzugake, several attackers, at a seminar in Pardubice, Czech Republic. Photo by Leos Matousek.

"In the beginning was the Word, and the Word was with God, and the Word was God." The power of words is also evident in Genesis, where God creates the world by simply ordering it to appear, bit by bit, with the phrase: "Let there be..."

Perhaps the underlying thoughts of kototama come from the Tantric teaching *sphota-vada*, which was introduced to Japan by the Buddhist priest Kukai in the 9th century. He formed the Buddhist movement *Shingon*, the Word of Truth, which still exists. The word shingon means the same as the Indian Sanskrit word *mantra*, referring to holy words that lead man to clarity and a higher consciousness, when pronounced.

The most well known mantra is *OM*, the universal, written with a symbol that contains the letters A, U, and M. When you meditate on the mantra OM, the sound shall rise from the bottom of the abdomen all the way to the top of the head, while the sound glides from O to M. A classical Indian phrase is *Om mani padme hum*: Om, the jewel, has appeared in the world. This perspective is quite near that of kototama.

Kototama had a kind of renaissance in the beginning of the 20th century inside some religious movements, such as Omotokyo. Some of these movements – though not Omoto-kyo, which had a strikingly tolerant and open-minded world view – saw this cosmology as confirmation of the superiority of the Japanese language. When the Japanese emperor surrendered to the American forces, at the end of World War II, then Japanese disappointment and shame made Shinto lose its importance, thereby also kototama.

Today very few aikido instructors are familiar with kototama, or show any interest in the system. Neither former doshu Kisshomaru Ueshiba, nor present doshu Moriteru Ueshiba, seem to have given kototama any particular significance in aikido. Others have done so. The former shihan of Swedish aikido, Toshikazu Ichimura, studied and taught kototama intensely, until he entered a Japanese Christian movement. So did Masahilo Nakazono (1918-1994), who taught aikido in France in the 1960's, and moved to USA in

The order of the kototama sounds.

the early 1970's. In the US he soon quit aikido completely, to focus on kototama and natural medicine.

I believe that also the noble teacher Rinjiro Shirata (1912-1993) was well acquainted with kototama, and surely some others of Osensei's direct students.

Although kototama plays no visible role in aikido or other budo arts, it is there so to speak behind the scenes. Many *kiai* seem to be linked to kototama principles, also substantial parts of the cosmology that aikido and other budo arts imply and express. Therefore, let us have a look at this intricate teaching.

Object and subject

The Japanese Shinto source *Kojiki*, The Records of Ancient Matters, from the 8th century, tells about how the sun goddess Amaterasu once was so upset by the malice of the world that she ran and hid in a cave. The world was darkened, and the other gods did not know how to bring the light back. They gathered at the entrance of the cave and begged Amaterasu to have pity on the world and return to it, but she refused to comply.

Then they got the idea of luring her out with a mirror. They held it up to Amaterasu, so that she could see herself in it. She got so curious of her own reflection, and delighted by seeing something that pure and brilliant in the world she had renounced, she finally got out of the cave to have a closer look. The light returned to the world.

This tale is one of the most central of the religious legends of Japan, which calls itself the realm of the sun. And there is great symbolism in the goddess' meeting with her own reflection, bringing about the light.

Kototama regards the cosmos as two-sided: what is, and its expression. Object and subject. What is has no limitation, but no substance until it is noticeable, until it reflects itself and becomes aware of itself. Accordingly, man exists through what he does, the imprints he makes on the world. Each human being gets to know himself by becoming aware of his own actions, his body, his thoughts, and emotions. Our conscious mind is what makes our being tangible, what makes us real.

Creation

Kototama explains the emergence of the universe in the same way. At first, there was only chaos, the great darkness, which existed but could neither be perceived nor experienced. When there was light, its reflection was born at the same time – the observation of the light. What light would there be, without an eye to see it?

Kototama describes this process with sounds, where the primordial dark chaos is U, which corresponds to the Shinto god Ameno-Minaka-Nusi. The observer is the sound A, the god Takami-Musubi, and the observed is the sound WA, the god Kami-Musubi. When the observing force A has been born, two must follow it: the memory of the observed, which is the sound O, and the conclusion, the judgment of the observed, which is the sound E. From the observed side WA, WO and WE are simultaneously born.

Out of these four of the third generation of creation, eight new forces emerge – two from each of the four. They

	N	Y	R	M	K	S	T	H	
I	NI	YI	RI	MI	KI	SI	TI	HI	**WI**
E	NE	YE	RE	ME	KE	SE	TE	HE	**WE**
A	NA	YA	RA	MA	KA	SA	TA	HA	**WA**
O	NO	YO	RO	MO	KO	SO	TO	HO	**WO**
U	NU	YU	RU	MU	KU	SU	TU	HU	**WU**

The 50 basic kototama words.

are the consonants of kototama: N, Y, R, M, K, S, T, and H. Kototama regards Y as a consonant, pronouncing it quite the same as the English Y in such words as you or young.

Finally, there is a life force permeating all this, an ether without borders, enclosing all the other forces and making them a whole. Its active substance is the word I, represented by the god Izanagi, and its passive object side is the sound WI, the god Izanami. These two gods were twins, male and female, who were quite instrumental in the creation of the world. They stirred the sea and thereby raised the mud from its bottom that became Japan. It was out of their incestuous marriage that the Imperial family was born, according to the myths.

From this principle of creation, the words are sorted into a system, where the vowels are called mothers, the consonants fathers, and the combinations of them are the children. A diagram of the sounds shows a total of fifty basic one-syllable words: the five vowels, their five mirrors, and the forty combinations of vowels and consonants. If all the fifty words are united into one, this is WN, which stands for the all of the universe.

Sounds that are not included in this system, such as the Scandinavian vowels Ä and Ö, as well as a number of consonants, are by kototama regarded as impure sounds, invented by mankind. Such sounds are not condemned, but they do not carry the spiritual meaning described by kototama.

Among the left out consonants is L, but the Japanese language does not separate L from R, which is included. D,

Aikido

G, and Z are also missing, but their unvoiced counterparts T, K, and S are not. On the other hand, both the voiced consonant B and the unvoiced P are missing, although they do exist – rarely – in the Japanese language. There may be another phonetic explanation somewhere.

Hidden

Nakazono and his kototama teacher Koji Ogasawara (1903-1982) claimed that the kototama principles were hidden to mankind when they lived in *Takamahara*, a sort of Eden. This was done so that man should struggle to explore the world, and through this deepened contemplation of it make it whole, by proving the world to itself.

This mapping and investigation of the world has been going on for four thousand years. There is soon time for us to come across the basic evidence of the existence of kototama, and then a third era will commence. Nakazono studied *Takeuti Kobunken*, a Shinto classic, and concluded that it will happen in the year 2011. By then we have found confirmations of the religious principles, and we settle in a world of peace, which is whole and observes itself in its wholeness.

The thought that sounds or vibrations could be connected to the laws and forces of the universe is not necessarily that farfetched. Kototama practitioners of today refer to discoveries within the science of physics that point in the same direction. Light consists of waves, and so does sound – although of a much slower kind. Atoms contain particle movement, and the whole cosmos is full of all kinds of radiation. Practically everything in the universe consists of periodic movement – i.e. vibrations.

The question is if something that does not move can exist at all.

We talk about the absolute zero temperature (-459.67° Fahrenheit, -273.16° Celsius) as a cold where atomic movement has stopped completely. It has not been measured anywhere. Nothing in the world wants to be completely still. Actually, since matter is a form of energy, it would cease to exist if its movement halted altogether.

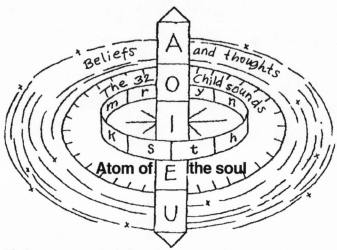

The kototama cosmological gyroscope.

In kototama, this basic principle of eternal movement is complemented with theories about the significance of certain vibrations and sounds. Certainly, this is intimately linked to language, and to the emotions and associations that different sounds generate in us when we pronounce them. Although it is all based on Japanese language and pronunciation, it is not that difficult to see the reasoning and experience behind it.

The vowels
The five vowels describe stages in human evolution. The same stages can be found in the development of civilization.

U is the first stage. It is pronounced like in 'human' or 'you'. This is the basic stage, which deals with survival and procreation. Only strictly concrete matters have an appeal on this level, which is focused on production and fortune.

O, pronounced as in 'order' or 'source', is the constructive stage, signified by engineering, inventions, and progress. Ambition rules, everyday life gets organized, buildings are erected, and technology advances. Natural science rules the thoughts.

A, pronounced as the first vowel sound in 'sigh' or 'my', is the reflecting stage, where existence is contemplated and portrayed. The longings for meaning and beauty grow. Art and religion belong to this stage, as do the emotions.

E, pronounced as in 'ethics', actually is the ethical stage. On this level the previous stages can be seen clearly. Their traits and purposes can be judged. Right and wrong, good and bad, are possible to perceive. The moral principles and man's mission in life are considered.

I, pronounced as in 'see' or 'bee', is the very life force that permeates everything. Only when this stage is reached, all the pieces of the puzzle fall into place. One can realize one's insights, and integrate them with one's life. Broodings of earlier stages lose their meaning. Everything is clear, and man is both complete and born anew. This highest stage is in itself nothing new. It brings life into all the experiences of the previous stages, and puts them in the right perspective.

Kiai

Several common *kiai* can be depicted as directions in this evolutionary ladder. UI, which was the kiai used by my former teacher Toshikazu Ichimura, describes the whole ladder from its base to its top. It is a kiai to stimulate the movement upward, and to show that the movement made during the kiai lacks nothing.

EI, a very common kiai in traditional budo, contains the two top steps of the ladder, where the ethical stage is stressed and awakened to real life. This kiai expresses a moral right to the action in question, and a wish that it will lead to good, also to give life instead of stealing it.

Kiai that express the opposite direction on the ladder are not as common, especially not among Japanese practitioners. According to kototama they must be regarded as unfortunate. The one who likes to shout IA happens to reveal that by his technique he wants to constrain life to an art, which means that he has a narcissistic urge to show off his ability.

Notice that in the word for no, *iie*, which the Japanese

U	instinct	**N**	attracting
O	knowledge	**Y**	distancing
A	emotion	**R**	whirling
E	ethics	**M**	revolving
I	life		
WU	origin	**K**	scratching
WO	memory	**S**	piercing
WA	sense	**T**	spreading
WE	ideal	**H**	developing
WI	change		

The basic kototama sounds explained.

do not like to use, the vowels travel backward on the koto-tama ladder, but in yes, *hai*, they move upward.

The consonants

The consonants, which are called the father sounds, are not as easy to explain as the vowels. They are born in pairs out of O, WO, E, and WE, where the pure vowels O and E stand for the subjective active, and their opposites stand for the objective passive. This also goes for the consonants linked to them.

The first four – N, Y, R and M – belong to the passive side, with their softly extended sounds. The four on the active side – K, S, T, and H – are short and hard in tone, with the possible exception of S, but that sound has a sharpness that still makes it fit this group.

The consonants represent directions. Therefore they are meaningless until they carry something – as when they are combined with the vowels. N is attracting, Y is distancing, R is whirling, M is revolving, K is scratching, S is piercing, T is spreading, and H is developing. The first four are of the passive type, and the others of the active type.

Child sounds

When vowels and consonants form their children, each of them gets its own meaning, depending on the sounds it combines. These meanings are often abstract and hard to comprehend, as the teachers of kototama present them. Although the child sounds are supposed to be the most concrete expressions of the kototama principles, the explanations are as vague as if failing to decipher their meaning. We could compare it to the atoms, which seem to be increasingly incomprehensible to science the closer they are observed, and the smaller parts they are divided into.

Still, let us try to explain the workings of the kototama child sounds, by the use of a joyous example.

When we laugh, that sound can usually be described as the consonant H in combination with one or other vowel. That is how laughter sounds, and that is how we write it. In kototama, how we write sounds is regarded as of high symbolic value.

H always means to develop, like the flower when it blooms, or for that matter fire when it consumes. Laughter gushes forth from our interior. It is certainly of the subjective active kind. The choice of vowel reveals the character of the laughter, the spirit of it.

HI is the happy laughter, feeding on the delight of existing and being able to experience the fun, whatever it is. This laughter is like being tickled, or pleasantly drunk.

HE is the victorious laughter of the one who knows that he is right, who sees his plans realized, or who rejects others. This laughter does not have that much to do with joy, but with analysis and conclusion. It can often sound supercilious or even scornful.

HA is the big laughter where the sense of joy is completely released. Here the emotion is central – having fun and showing it. Such laughter must be loud and lasting. When the syllable is pronounced just once, it expresses pride and triumph.

HO is the laughter of Santa Claus, of course. The fat old man comes with presents, traveling all over the world to

Drawing from the 1970's by Berlin based artist and aikido instructor Mikael Eriksson.

spread some materialistic happiness. This is the laughter of someone who comes from somewhere and is going somewhere else, and who can allow himself to laugh on the way, but still does not interrupt the journey. It is a laughter that accompanies a pleasing process, but not one that erupts at the end of a joke.

HU is the deep laughter from man's dark interior. It preferably follows a horror story, or other ways of inducing fright. The feeling is obscure. It could be the sound of crying or grunting, just as well as that of laughing. The sound is difficult to interpret, and therefore worrying, far from jolly.

Of course, the above is little more than onomatopoetic simplification, like in comic strips, and should not be taken any more seriously. Nonetheless, speaking about comic strips, it is interesting that they have found simplifying expressions of human behavior and emotions that come close to the kototama principles.

Suitable kiai

Returning to the kiai of the budo arts, kototama principles point out the benefit of choosing kiai according to what you want to accomplish.

When in karatedo you want to practice *tameshiware*, breaking objects, a combination of S for the penetration and O for the technique, the constructive and the destructive, is the most suitable.

Oddly, many karate practitioners have the habit of greeting each other and responding to their instructor with a word that sounds like OS, the kototama meaning of which is to use one's technique in order to penetrate. The one who prefers to invigorate the one he hits should use SI as a kiai – to penetrate in order to give life, like the injection of medicine to an ailing patient.

In aikido, the consonants R and M, whirl and revolve, ought to be the most suitable. Also fitting is the artistic vowel A, which is also the first sound of the name of this martial art. Then it will become like a dance.

If you wish an aikido rooted in the principle of peacefulness, and fostering others to it, the vowel E is the obvious choice. But then the consonants must change from passive to active. Maybe KE to approach the partner and correct him or her, then TE to spread the forces and thereby put an end to the battle – that corresponds to the steps irimi and tenkan.

Another kototama way to perform irimi-tenkan is to start the spirit of penetrating the basic aggression of the attacker with SU, followed by TE to spread and transform the energy.

Kototama in aikido

Kototama is not only an abstract cosmology of vibrations. It can be practiced – either in itself, by chanting the sounds as a way of self-purification, or in aikido, in order to fill the techniques with meaning.

Aikido is usually practiced in silence, in spite of the fact that Osensei made sounds constantly in his aikido training. His students may have felt intimidated by the power his

Aikido drawing by Swedish artist Gisela Döhler.

intense sounds carried. Nevertheless, sounds can be used by both the attacker and the defender, and there is much to discover in the process.

The attacker should use a kiai that fits the attack's type and purpose. Starting in U brings up the animalistic fight for survival that is probably the very root of any aggression. UO takes this energy and uses it to power a technique, whether it is constructive or destructive. The O sound makes the attack concrete and its effect lasting.

Of course, other kiai work fine too, but UO is a basic starting point for the defender to work on, and try to transform.

The defender should make his or her sound relate to

that of the attacker. An UO attack needs to be corrected. The response should change the situation from one of hostility, into one of learning and development. A sudden *irimi* entrance and *atemi* strike done with IE takes the very power of life into scolding or even punishing the attacker for the mistake of hostility. It is a reprimand, a lesson to be learned.

If the kiai is EI, the sounds in reverse order, then the defender expresses his or her right to do away with the situation as it is, and create new life, a fresh start for both. Where IE arrests the situation, EI solves it and moves on. Both methods are worth studying.

Now, an aikido technique can be described by kototama to contain three stages: The initial chaos of the attacking spirit, which is like the world before its creation, then the transformation of that situation into one of beauty and creativity, and finally the moment when the attacker realizes the transformation and learns from it. This is like the process of the world creation, expressed by U-A-WA.

You can do any aikido technique with these three sounds, one after the other. U is the initial moment, when the attacker's spirit rules the situation. A is when the defender makes the *taisabaki* evasive movement and leads the attacker into a technique, without the latter realizing what is going on. WA is the throw in a *nage* or the end pinning in a *katame* technique, which is the moment when the attacker realizes what has happened.

You learn a lot by contemplating these three phases of any aikido technique, whether you make kototama sounds during it or not. The sounds will definitely help you discover these phases and refine them.

There are many other ways to use kototama in aikido practice, but the above ones are simple, and still quite rewarding. From then on, trust your center, and experiment.

Aikido in kototama

Of course, we have to analyze the word aikido with kototama. The first two vowels describe a movement from art and emotion to life itself – an art that should give life. That

Breathing exercise at a Berlin seminar. Photo by Frank Weingärtner.

was no doubt Osensei's wish. Ki is the force, something that touches on life itself, and thereby constantly stimulates it. DO does in kototama become TO, which signifies spreading knowledge and ability. Then the whole concept of aikido can be explained as: spreading knowledge about how to stimulate life itself into making a lively art.

Such a study is worth a lifetime. Expressed in kototama it also clearly shows a value reaching far beyond the dojo walls. Anything less would not have attracted people to aikido practice year after year, decade after decade. Most of those who have trained aikido for that long can give you no answer as to why, what is keeping them. Maybe kototama has the answer, and maybe not.

Nonetheless, I have noticed that its principles make for inspiring exercises in aikido practice, and stimulate new approaches – especially to those who have done aikido the longest.

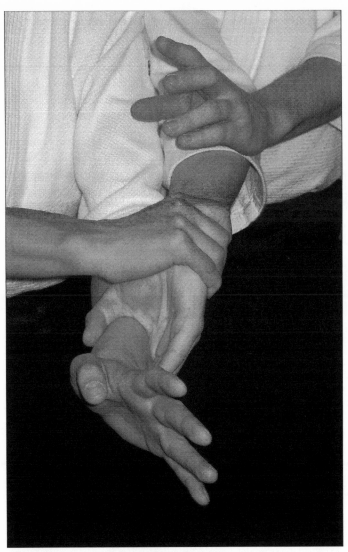

Shihonage entrance. Photo by the author.

Appendix

Osensei's rules for training aikido

When the number of practitioners increased at Morihei Ueshiba's dojo, some of the senior students asked him if there should be some rules for training. He was not that much into regulations, so he smiled at them and said: "So, times have changed!"

Then he quickly wrote down the six guidelines below. This was around 1935, and since then the rules have been called approximately *Reminders in Aikido Practice*. They may seem a bit dramatic in their choice of words, here and there, but are still used as a guide for each aikidoist. Former doshu Kisshomaru Ueshiba, the son of Osensei, suggested a modern version of the rules – the addendum below.

The texts are from Kisshomaru Ueshiba's book *The Spirit of Aikido*, originally published in 1984.

Reminders in Aikido Practice

1   Aikido decides life and death in a single strike, so students must carefully follow the instructor's teaching and not compete to see who is the strongest.

2   Aikido is the way that teaches how one can deal with several enemies. Students must train themselves to be alert not just to the front, but to all sides and the back.

3   Training should always be conducted in a pleasant and joyful atmosphere.

4   The instructor teaches only one small aspect of the art. Its versatile applications must be discovered by each student through incessant practice and training.

5   In daily practice first begin by moving your body [Osensei referred specifically to the *tai no tenkan/tai no henko* exercise] and then progress to more intensive practice. Never force anything unnaturally or unreasonably. If this rule is followed, then even elderly people will not hurt themselves and they can train in a pleasant and joyful atmosphere.

6   The purpose of aikido is to train mind and body and to produce sincere, earnest people. Since all the techniques are

Yasuo Kobayashi, 8 dan Aikikai shihan, at a Stockholm seminar. Photo by Magnus Hartman.

to be transmitted person-to-person, do not randomly reveal them to others, for this might lead to their being used by hoodlums.

Addendum to the rules, by Kisshomaru Ueshiba

1   Proper aikido can never be mastered unless one strictly follows the instructor's teaching.

2   Aikido as a martial art is perfected by being alert to everything going on around us and leaving no vulnerable opening (*suki*).

3   Practice becomes joyful and pleasant once one has trained enough not to be bothered by pain.

4   Do not be satisfied by what is taught at the dojo. One must constantly digest, experiment and develop what one has learned.

5   One should never force things unnaturally or unreasonably in practice. One should undertake training suited to one's body, physical condition, and age.

6   The aim of aikido is to develop the truly human self. It should not be used to display ego.

Budo Charter – the Japanese rules

In 1987, the Japanese Budo Association (*Nippon Budo Shingikai*) established a Charter of budo, the Japanese martial arts. It consists of six articles to serve as guidelines for how budo practice should be carried out. The work on this Charter had taken six years, with lectures and meetings in big committees. The aikido representative was former doshu Kisshomaru Ueshiba.

The Japanese Budo Association is a loosely formed association of the independent Japanese organizations of judo, kendo, kyudo, sumo, karatedo, aikido, kempo, naginata, jukendo, and Nippon Budokan.

The Budo Charter

Budo, rooted in the martial spirit of ancient Japan, is an aspect of traditional culture that has evolved from *jutsu* to *do* through centuries of historical and social change.

Following the concept of unity of mind and technique, budo has developed and refined a discipline of austere training, which promotes etiquette, skillful technique, physical strength, and the unity of mind and body. Modern Japanese have inherited these values and they play a prominent role in forming Japanese personalities. In modern Japan the budo spirit is a source of powerful energy and promotes a pleasant disposition in the individual.

Today, budo has been diffused throughout the world and has attracted strong interest internationally. However, infatuation with mere technical training and undue concern with winning are severe threats to the essence of budo. To prevent this perversion of the art, we must continually examine ourselves and endeavor to perfect and preserve this national heritage.

It is with this hope that we establish the Budo Charter in order to uphold the fundamental principles of traditional budo.

1 Object
The object of budo is to cultivate character, enrich the ability to make value judgments, and foster a well-disciplined and capable individual through participation in physical and mental training utilizing martial techniques.

2 Keiko
When practicing daily, one must constantly follow decorum, adhere to the fundamentals, and resist the temptation to pursue mere technical skill rather than the unity of mind and technique.

3 Shiai
In a match and the performance of kata, one must manifest budo spirit, exert oneself to the utmost, win with modesty, accept defeat gracefully, and constantly exhibit temperate attitudes.

4 Dojo
The dojo is a sacred place for training one's mind and body. Here, one must maintain discipline, proper etiquette, and formality. The training area must be a quiet, clean, safe and solemn environment.

5 Teaching
When teaching trainees, in order to be an effective teacher, the budo master should always strive to cultivate his/her character, and further his/her own skill and discipline of mind and body. He/she should not be swayed by winning or losing, or display arrogance about his/her superior skill, but rather he/she should retain the attitudes suitable for a role model.

6 Promotion
When promoting budo, one should follow traditional values, seek substantial training, contribute to research, and do one's utmost to perfect and preserve this traditional art with an understanding of international points of view.

Aikibatto jo exercise at the author's dojo, with Tomas Ohlsson as uke.

Glossary of aikido terms

The aikido terminology is in Japanese. It's "all Greek" to the beginner, but by time we all learn most of it. Here is a comprised dictionary of aikido terms, with short translations and explanations.

A

ai harmony, unity, blending

aihanmi basic relation between partners: both have same foot forward (left or right), compare *gyakuhanmi*

aihanmi katatedori wrist grip, right on right or left on left, also called *kosadori*, compare *gyakuhanmi katatedori*

aiki blending/uniting one's ki with that of the partner

aikibatto sword exercises, solo or pair

aikibudo budo based on the aiki principle, earlier name for aikido

aikido the way through the life energy to harmony/unity

aikidoka one who does aikido, specifically on an advanced or professional level

aikido toho Nishio sensei's iaido school

Aikijinja the aikido temple in Iwama

aikijo aikido jo-staff exercises

aikijutsu name on the Daito ryu martial art, also called *aikijujutsu*

Aikikai organization and "label" for Morihei Ueshiba's aikido

aikiken aikido sword exercises

aikinage aiki-throw, throwing technique

aiki no michi aikido (michi=do)

aikiotoshi aiki-drop, throwing technique

aikitaiso aikido warm-up exercises

aite partner in training

arigato thanks

arigato gozaimasu thanks for something going on

arigato gozaimashita thanks for something completed

ashi leg, foot

ate hit, strike
atemi strike to the body
awase harmonizing/blending movement
ayumiashi altering steps, left and right, like normal walking, compare *tsugiashi*

B
barai/harai parry, ward off
batto draw the sword, also called *nuki*
bo staff, longer than the *jo*
bokken wooden training sword
bokuto same as *bokken*
bu war, battle, fight
budo the way of war/battle, the Japanese martial arts
budoka one who does any budo, specifically on an advanced or professional level
bugei battle art, old term
bukiwaza weapons training
bushi warrior
bushido the way of the warrior

C
chado tea ceremony
chikara force/strength
choku direct
chokutsuki direct strike with the *jo*
chudan middle, compare *jodan* and *gedan*
chudankamae guard position with a weapon at belly height
chudantsuki strike at belly/solar plexus, with weapon or empty hand
chukyusha continuing student, with a mid-level kyu grade, compare *jokyusha*

D
dai big, also o
daisho sword pair, the long and the short sword
Daito ryu *aikijutsu* school
dame wrong, bad

dan level, black belt grade in budo
dao/tao transcription of the Chinese word for way, *do*
deshi student
do way, also *michi*
dogi training dress, also *keikogi*
do-in self massage tradition
dojo training hall
dojo cho head of a training hall
doka poem about the way
domo much
domo arigato gozaimasu thank you so much, for something going on
domo arigato gozaimashita thank you so much, for something completed
dori take, catch, grab
dosa movement
doshu way leader, head of a budo art
dozo please/by all means

E
embukai public demonstration
empi strike with elbow
eri neck, collar
eridori collar grip by the neck

F
fukushidoin assisting instructor, title for aikido teacher, 2-3 dan, compare *shidoin* and *shihan*
funakogi undo, rowing exercise, also called *torifune*
furitama exercise to still ki
futaridori/futarigake two attackers

G
gaeshi/kaeshi returning, reversed
gamae/kamae guard, basic position
gasshuku training camp, lodging together
gedan low, compare *jodan* and *chudan*
gedanbarai low block

geiko/keiko training
geri kick
gi dress, as in *dogi* or *keikogi*
giri/kiri cut
go five
gokyo fifth teaching, pinning technique
gomen nasai excuse me
Gorin no sho *Book of Five Rings*, book written by Miyamoto Musashi in the 17th century
gotai/kotai hard body, static training, compare *jutai*, *ryutai*, and *kinagare*
gyaku reverse, opposite
gyakuhanmi basic relation between partners: they have opposite foot forward, compare *aihanmi*
gyakuhanmi katatedori wrist grip, right on left or left on right, compare *aihanmi katatedori*
gyakutsuki strike with opposing arm and leg forward, compare *oitsuki*

H
hachi eight
Hagakure *Hiding the Leaves*, classic samurai book from the 18th century
hai yes
hajime begin
hakama traditional wide pants, used in aikido
handachi half standing
hanmi half body
hanmigamae angled guard position
hanmi handachiwaza sitting versus standing
hanshi title in kendo, from 8th dan, compare *renshi* and *kyushi*
hantai opposed
happo eight directions, compare *shiho*
hara stomach
harai/barai sweep away, parry
harakiri cut belly, ritual suicide, also called *seppuku*
hassogaeshi *jo* staff technique

hassogamae guard with weapon at shoulder level
henkawaza, changing techniques, variations on basic techniques, also shifting from one technique to another
hidari left (right: *migi*)
hiji elbow
hijidori grip on elbow
hijikimeosae pinning technique, sometimes called *rokkyo*
hiki pull
hineri twist
hiragana Japanese phonetic writing, compare *katakana*
hito e mi making the body small, guard position with more of an angle than *hanmi*
hiza knee
ho method
ho direction, side
hombu head quarters
Hombu dojo head dojo, used for the Aikikai head dojo in Tokyo

I

iaido the art of drawing the Japanese sword
iaito training sword, usually not sharpened
ichi one
ichiban first, best
iie no
iki willpower
ikkajo older term for *ikkyo*
ikki one *ki*, bottoms up, toast
ikkyo first teaching, pinning technique
ikkyo undo exercise of the basic *ikkyo* movement
in Japanese for the Chinese concept *yin*, compare *yo*
ippon one point
ipponken strike with one knuckle
irimi in to the body, inward, compare *tenkan*
iriminage inward throw, throwing technique
Iwama Japanese town, where Osensei had a dojo and a home
Iwama ryu Saito sensei's aikido style

J

jiyuwaza free training
jo wooden staff, 127.5 centimeters
jo awase *jo* staff exercises
jodan high, compare *chudan* and *gedan*
jodankamae guard with weapon over head
jodantsuki strike at head
jodanuke high block
jodo the way of the staff
jodori defense against *jo* staff
jokyusha advanced student, with a higher kyu grade, compare *chukyusha*
ju ten
ju soft
judo the soft way, or the way to softness
jujigarami/jujinage cross throw
jujutsu the soft art
jumbitaiso warm-up exercises, also called *aikitaiso*
juntsuki strike with the same arm and leg forward, also called *oitsuki*, compare *gyakutsuki*
jutai soft body, smooth training, compare *gotai, ryutai,* and *kinagare*
jutsu technique or art

K

kaeshi/gaeshi returning, reverse
kaeshitsuki reverse strike with *jo* staff
kaeshiwaza counter techniques
kagamibiraki Japanese New Year celebration, held January 11
kai club, association
kaiso founder
kaitennage rotation throw, throwing technique
kaitenosae rotation pinning technique
kakaedori embrace
kakarigeiko attackers in line, one after the other
kakudo angle
kamae/gamae guard position

Mutsuko Minegishi, 6 dan Aikikai shihan, at a Stockholm seminar. Photo by Magnus Hartman.

kami divinity

kamiza honorary place in a dojo, compare *shomen* and *shinzen*

kampai cheers, toast

kan intuition

kangeiko mid-winter training

kanji ideograms, the Chinese writing

kanren linked, connected

kanrenwaza linked techniques, one technique followed by another, compare *renzokuwaza*

kansetsu joint on body

karatedo the way of the empty hand, or the way through the hand to emptiness

Kashima shintoryu traditional sword school

kata form, pre-decided movements

kata shoulder

katadori shoulder grip

katadori menuchi shoulder grip followed by *shomenuchi*

katakana Japanese phonetic writing, compare *hiragana*

katamewaza pinning techniques

katana the Japanese sword, also *ken*, *to*, and *tachi*

katate one-handed technique
katatedori wrist grip
katate ryotedori grip with both hands, also called *morotedori*
Katori shintoryu traditional sword school
keiko/geiko training
keikogi training dress, also *dogi*
ken sword, also *katana*, *to*, and *tachi*
kendo Japanese fencing
ki spirit, life energy
kiai gathered *ki*, usually used for shout in budo
ki-aikido Tohei sensei's aikido style
kihon basics
kihonwaza basic training
kikai tanden the ocean of *ki* in the body's center
kime focusing
kimusubi tying one's *ki* to that of the partner
kinagare/ki no nagare streaming ki, flowing training, compare *gotai*, *jutai*, and *ryutai*
Ki no kenkyukai Tohei sensei's aikido school, also *Shinshin toitsu*
kiri/giri cut
kirikaeshi turning cut, sword exercise
koan riddle in *Zen*
kobudo older budo
kogeki attack
kogekiho attack techniques
kohai one's junior, compare *sempai*
Kojiki religious Japanese book from the 8th century
kokoro heart, will, mind, also pronounced *shin*
kokyu breathing
kokyuho breathing exercise, throwing technique
kokyunage breath throw
kokyu ryoku breath power
kosa cross over, pass
kosadori cross-over grip, same as *aihanmi katatedori*
koshi hip
koshinage hip throw
kotai see *gotai*

kote wrist
kotegaeshi reversed wrist, throwing technique
kotehineri twisted wrist, *sankyo*
kotemawashi turned wrist, *nikyo*
kotodama/kototama spirit of words, Japanese cosmology based on sounds
ku nine
ku emptiness
kubi neck
kubishime neck choke
kuden oral tradition or teaching
kumi group, set
kumijo *jo* staff exercises, jo against jo
kumitachi sword exercises, sword against sword
kumite empty handed fight
kumiuchi ancient Japanese wrestling in full armor
kuzushi break balance
kyo principle, learning
kyoshi title in kendo, 6-7 dan, compare *renshi* and *hanshi*
kyu grade before blackbelt, compare *dan*
kyudo the way of the bow and arrow

L
(L not used in Japanese)

M
ma distance between training partners
maai harmonious, balanced distance between training partners
mae front, forward, compare *ushiro*
maegeri straight kick
mae ukemi forward fall, compare *ushiro ukemi*
makiwara target for hitting practice in karatedo
maru circle
mawashi revolving, turning
mawashigeri roundhouse kick
mawate turning
me eye

men head
michi way, also *do*
migi right (left: *hidari*)
misogi purification, cleansing
mochi hold or grip, also called *dori*
mochikata gripping attacks
mo ikkai do again
mokuso meditation, also called *zazen*
moro both
morotedori grip with both hands, also called *katate ryotedori*
mu nothing, empty
mushin empty mind
mudansha trainee without dan grade, compare *yudansha*
mune chest
munedori collar grip by the chest
musubi tie together

N
nagare flow, streaming
nage throw, also used for the one doing the aikido technique, compare *tori*
nagewaza throwing techniques
naginata Japanese halberd
nakaima here and now
nana seven, also pronounced *shichi*
nen the purity and unity of the mind
ni two
Nihon/Nippon Japan
Nihongi religious Japanese book from the 8th century
nikajo older name for *nikyo*
nikyo second teaching, pinning technique
nin person
ninindori two attackers, also called *futaridori*
ninja courier and spy in old Japan
Nippon/Nihon Japan
Nito ichiryu/Niten ichiryu School of Two Swords/Two Heavens, Miyamoto Musashi's sword school
noto return the sword to the scabbard

Toshikazu Ichimura, 6 dan Aikikai and 6 dan renshi iaido, at a iaido class in the early 1970's. He was the national aikido instructor of Sweden 1966-86. Photo by the author.

nuki draw the sword, also called *batto*
nukite strike with fingertips

O
o big, also *dai*
obi belt
ocha tea
oitsuki strike with same arm and foot forward, also called *jontsuki*
omote front, surface, compare *ura*
Omotokyo a Shinto society
onegai shimasu please, asking for something
osae press down, pinning
osensei great teacher, in aikido Morihei Ueshiba
otagai ni rei bow to each others
otoshi drop
oyowaza applied techniques, modified for efficiency

P
(P rarely used in Japanese)

Q
(Q not used in Japanese)

R
randori disorderly grabbing, free training
rei bow
reigi etiquette, also called *reishiki*
renshi title in kendo, 4-6 dan, compare *hanshi* and *kyoshi*
renshu training
renzoku continuous
renzoku uchikomi *jo* staff exercise
renzokuwaza consecutive techniques, a series of techniques
ritsurei standing bow
rokkyo sixth teaching, pinning technique, see *hijikime osae*
roku six
ryo both
ryotedori gripping both wrists
ryu school
ryutai flowing body, fluid training, compare *gotai*, *jutai*, and
kinagare

S
sabaki action or handling
sake rice wine
samurai to serve, Japanese warrior class
san three
sankajo older term for *sankyo*
sankaku triangle
sankakutai triangle shape, position of the feet in *hanmi*
sankyo third teaching, pinning technique
sannindori/sanningake three attackers
sanpo three directions
satori enlightenment in *Zen*
saya scabbard
seika no itten, the one point below the navel, the body cen-

ter, also called *tanden*
seiki life energy
seiza correct sitting, sit on knees
sempai one's senior, compare *kohai*
sen no sen before the attack, countering before the strike
sensei teacher
sensen no sen before before the attack, a leading initiative
seppuku cut belly, ritual suicide with sword, also called *harakiri*
shi four, also pronounced *yon*
shiai competition
shiatsu massage
shichi seven, also pronounced *nana*
shidoin instructor, middle title for aikido teacher, 4-5 dan, compare *fukushidoin* and *shihan*
shihan expert example, high title for aikido teacher, from 6 dan, compare *fukushidoin* and *shidoin*
shiho four directions
shihonage four directions throw, throwing technique
shikaku square
shikaku dead angle
shiki courage
shikko knee walking
shime choke
shin heart, will, mind, also pronounced *kokoro*
shinai kendo sword of bamboo
Shindo Musoryu *jodo* school
shinken sharp authentic Japanese sword
Shinshin toitsu Tohei sensei's aikido school, *Ki no kenkyukai*
Shinto the way of the gods, Japanese religion
shinzen seat of the gods, in a dojo usually a position on the wall farthest from the entrance, compare *kamiza* and *shomen*
shisei posture
shite the one leading, defender in aikido, also called *tori* or *nage*
shizentai natural body posture
sho first, beginning
shodan first dan grade

shodo calligraphy
Shodokan Tomiki sensei's aikido school
shomen front of the head
shomen head place of the dojo, compare *shinzen* and *kamiza*
shomen ni rei bow to head place of the dojo
shomenuchi strike to head
shoshinsha beginner
shuto hand ridge strike
sode sleeve
sodedori sleeve grip
sodeguchidori grip on the cuff of the sleeve
soto outside, outer, compare *uchi*
sotodeshi student who lives outside the dojo, compare *uchi-deshi*
sotokaiten outer rotation, compare *uchikaiten*
sotouke block from outside, compare *uchiuke*
suburi basic exercises with sword or staff
suki opening
sumi corner
sumikiri sharpness of body and mind
sumimasen excuse me
sumo traditional Japanese wrestling
suri rub, scrape
sutemiwaza techniques with losing one's own balance
suwariwaza seated training, also called *suwate*
suwate seated training, also called *suwariwaza*

T
tachi sword, also *to*, *ken*, and *katana*
tachi standing
tachidori defense against sword
tachiwaza training standing up
tai body
taijutsu body techniques, unarmed techniques
tai no henko body turn, also called *tai no tenkan*
tai no tenkan body turn, also called *tai no henko*
taisabaki body move, evasive movement in aikido
taiso exercises

Mikael Eriksson teaching a children's class in the early 1970's at Järfälla, Sweden. Photo by the author.

takemusu improvised martial art
takemusu aiki improvised martial art through the principle of *aiki*
tambo short staff
tameshi test
tameshigiri cutting test with sword
tameshiware hitting test in karatedo
tanden body center, compare *seika no itten*
taninzugake several attackers
tanren drill
tanto/tanken knife
tantodori defense against knife
tao/dao Chinese for *do*
tatami mat
tate stand up
te hand
tegatana hand sword, hand ridge in sword like movements
tekubi wrist
tekubiosae pinned wrist, *yonkyo*
tenchinage heaven-earth throw, throwing technique

tenkan turn
tettsui hammer strike
to sword, also *ken*, *tachi*, and *katana*
tobigeri jump kick
tobikoshi fall over hip, break fall
tomauchi *jo* staff technique
tori the one who takes, defender in aikido, also called *nage* and *shite*
torifune rowing exercise, also called *funakogi undo*
tsuba sword guard
tsugiashi following step, back foot following and not passing front foot, compare *ayumiashi*
tsuka sword hilt
tsuki strike, with a weapon or empty hand

U
uchi hit
uchi inside, within, inner, compare *soto*
uchideshi student living in the dojo, compare *sotodeshi*
uchikaiten inner rotation, compare *sotokaiten*
uchikata striking and hitting attack forms
uchikomi hitting repeatedly
uchiuke block from inside, compare *sotouke*
ude arm
udekimenage arm lock throw
udenobashi extended arm, *gokyo*
udeosae pinned arm, *ikkyo*
uke the one receiving, attacker in aikido
uke block, parry
ukemi falling
undo exercise
ura backside, inside, reverse side, compare *omote*
uraken backhand strike
ushiro behind, backwards, compare *mae*
ushirogeri backward kick
ushiro kiriotoshi rear cutting drop, throwing technique
ushiro ukemi backward fall, compare *mae ukemi*
ushirowaza attacks from behind

V

(V not used in Japanese)

W

waka sensei young teacher, used in aikido for the successor of *doshu*
waki side
wakizashi short sword
ware break, split
waza technique, skill, training method

X

(X not used in Japanese)

Y

yame stop
yang sunny side, male pole, in Japanese *yo*, compare *yin*
yari spear
yawara old *jujutsu*
yin shady side, female pole, in Japanese *in*, compare *yang*
yo Japanese for *yang*
yoko side, sideways, horizontal
yokogeri side kick
yokogiri side cut
yokomen side of the head
yokomenuchi strike to the side of the head
yoko ukemi side fall
yon four, also pronounced *shi*
yonkajo older term for *yonkyo*
yonkyo fourth teaching, pinning technique
Yoseikan Mochizuki sensei's aikido school
Yoshinkan Shioda sensei's aikido school
yudansha dan graded, compare *mudansha*

Z

za seated, sit
Zaidan Hojin Aikikai Aikikai Foundation
zanshin remaining spirit, continued concentration

Zazen at a demonstration in Brandbergen, Sweden, in the early 1980's.

zarei sitting bow
zazen sitting meditation, also called *mokuso*
Zen a form of buddhism
zengo around, forward and back, front and rear
zori sandals

Numbers
1   ichi
2   ni
3   san
4   shi / yon
5   go
6   roku
7   shichi / nana
8   hachi
9   ku
10   ju
20   ni-ju
21   ni-ju-ichi
100   hyaku
1000   sen

Aikido websites

I have an aikido website that contains quite a lot of material not included in this book. Among other things, I describe a number of aikido techniques in some detail. I have also posted video clips of them. Occasionally, I add things to the website – usually focusing more on aikido practice than on theory. Here it is:

www.stenudd.com/aikido

There is a lot about aikido on the internet, of course. Here are some website I can recommend. Most of them you probably already know about.

www.aikikai.or.jp is the website of Aikikai Hombu dojo in Tokyo, with information about that dojo and about the rules of the Aikikai system.

www.aikiweb.com is Jun Akiyama's very extensive website about aikido, also containing a lively forum that is the biggest about aikido on the internet.

www.aikidojournal.com is Stanley Pranin's big website, full of material from the many years of his work with Aiki News / Aikido Journal. It also contains his trustworthy Aikido Encyclopedia, and a very active forum.

www.aikidofaq.com is the old aikido FAQ by Kjartan Clausen. He has not updated it in a while, but it is still filled with interesting aikido material.

www.aikido-international.org is the website of the International Aikido Federation. It includes links to many national federations of aikido.

www.budo.net/Enighet is the website of my own dojo Enighet in Malmö, Sweden. Some of it is in English, but most of the updates are in Swedish only.

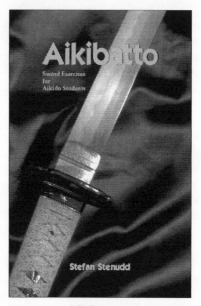

Aikibatto

Stefan Stenudd has also written a book about aikibatto, a system of sword and staff exercises for aikido students. You can find it at Amazon and other internet bookstores.

ISBN 978-1-4196-5878-5

2156726

Made in the USA